THE YEAR OF THE ROSE

The Daily Telegraph

THE YEAR OF THE ROSE

ENGLAND'S GRAND SLAM '91

EDITED BY Barrie Fairall

FOREWORD BY
Bill Beaumont

MAINSTREAM PUBLISHING
EDINBURGH AND LONDON

First published in Great Britain 1991 by
MAINSTREAM PUBLISHING COMPANY (EDINBURGH) LTD
7 Albany Street Edinburgh EH1 3UG

British Library Cataloguing in Publication Data

The Year of the Rose:
The Daily Telegraph Book of England's Grand Slam '91
1. England. Rugby Union Football
I. Fairall, Barrie
796.3330942

ISBN 1-85158-441-2

Typeset in 11/13 Garamond by
Falcon Typographic Art Ltd, Edinburgh and London
Printed in Great Britain by Butler and Tanner, Frome, Somerset

All pictures by
Colin Elsey and Andrew Cowie of Colorsport

To Will Carling and the England team
for delivering a great winning message
to English rugby after the long years of waiting.

ACKNOWLEDGMENTS

IN RUGBY, it is the teamwork that counts and when the whistle blew at tea-time on 16 March to signal England's Grand Slam, it was another team who swung into action to produce this book. Let us just say that the commitment shown off the field by all contributors and those working at Mainstream Publishing was also mighty impressive.

Michael Pearey, the Rugby Football Union's president, fired off his message and hit the target and Bill Beaumont, the sound of ringing in his ears, picked up the car phone.

Meanwhile, the *Telegraph* staffmen were limbering up and in poured the copy from John Mason, John Reason, Michael Calvin and Graham Tait. Backing these boys up came Jamie Salmon (I've never had to write 2,000 words before), Chris Jones, whose idea of recovering from glandular fever is to tap out a column before breakfast, Brendan Gallagher, who must secretly have been in full training, and David Llewellyn, whose phone bill must be horrendous.

Thanks are also due to Colorsport. They had the photographs on the way to the Mainstream office in Edinburgh in the time it takes you or I to load a film in a camera. And without the help and co-operation of those at *The Guardian*, *The Independent*, *The Independent on Sunday*, the *Mail on Sunday*, *The Observer*, and *The Sunday Times* and *Times*, the picture would definitely have been incomplete.

Contents

MESSAGE FROM THE PRESIDENT OF THE RUGBY FOOTBALL UNION

CAPTAIN MICHAEL PEAREY RN

IT GIVES ME GREAT PLEASURE to write a short message in this, England's Grand Slam year.

Rugby is a hard, competitive contact game demanding high skills in running and passing, supreme fitness and endurance, strength and stamina, commitment and courage. We saw all these qualities in abundance this year. That England have triumphed reflects enormous credit on the team management and the players. They have been totally dedicated, they have given their all, they are a pleasure to know, they deserve to be champions. England salutes them.

What a tournament. In their first match, England had to overcome 28 years of history, and the Cardiff bogey, against a young Welsh side that showed grit, courage, a superb defence, a willingness to have a go and commitment. Scotland, last season's champions, who flew the flag for rugby in the northern hemisphere with such distinction in New Zealand, possessed skill and experience and played the game at tremendous pace, with no quarter asked nor given. For 75 minutes the warm, welcoming men of Ireland tore around Lansdowne Road, consuming every Englishman in sight. And France, in the grand finale at Twickenham, with both sides unbeaten and with the immortal Serge Blanco playing his last game in a Five Nations' Championship match, produced the imagination, the adventure, the innovativeness, the unpredictability, the pace and the running skills for which they are renowned. England, with remarkable single-mindedness, with skill and strength in every position, playing for each other, playing as a team, playing for England, soaked up the pressure, kept their cool, applied pressure themselves, imposed their will – and won.

Each and every game was different; all were hard. Above all they were played in the spirit of rugby football and, once the final whistle had blown, the friendship and camaraderie that permeates rugby football, that *is* rugby football, prevailed.

Thank you, England, for a great season. Thank you, France, Ireland, Scotland and Wales for many wonderful moments. May the friendships made and renewed this year through rugby football continue throughout our lives.

Thank you, *Daily Telegraph*, for producing this souvenir of a great season for England. We now look forward to the World Cup.

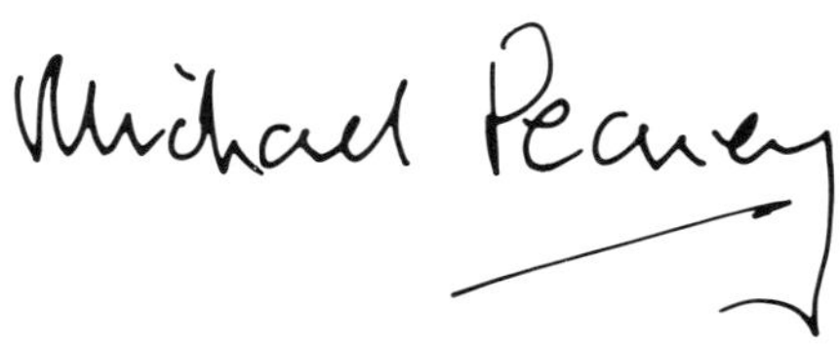

CAPTAIN MICHAEL PEAREY RN, PRESIDENT OF THE RFU

FOREWORD

By BILL BEAUMONT

WHAT A FANTASTIC ACHIEVEMENT by England to win the Championship and the Grand Slam. It is a really tremendous thing to do the Grand Slam by any stretch of the imagination. It doesn't matter what era you play in, to win all four games in the Five Nations' Championship really takes some doing. I salute Will Carling and his team. What they have done is outstanding – especially so when you consider how badly they came unstuck last season against Scotland at Murrayfield when they were favourites and it was the Scots who achieved the feat instead. And what about the season before when England had the chance of the Triple Crown? All they had to do was win in Cardiff. All they had to do!

In spite of all that, this year England again started favourites. From the outset of this year's Championship they were the side to beat and, in a way, that is a unique situation for a side that hasn't actually won anything for the last 11 years.

On the way to this marvellous Grand Slam England managed to lay to rest two ghosts. Thanks to a superb kicking performance by fullback Simon Hodgkinson no one will be able to say in future that England haven't won at Cardiff since 1963. That was an emphatic victory, wiping out 28 years of anguish for English supporters. I have to say I have never been more certain in my life that England were going to win an away game. I think they were in a strong position. They held a psychological edge over the Welsh after the victory at Twickenham last year. And really the poor state of Welsh rugby on the international field at the moment also contributed to my certainty.

The second ghost that was laid to rest was the spirit of 1980 and my own Grand Slam-winning team. All I can say is well done. I am absolutely delighted they have done it. As an ex-Grand Slam captain I think it is marvellous that England are back on top because ultimately I'm an Englishman and an England supporter through and through. I want to see England up there. I feel I was fortunate to have played in the era I did and was lucky enough to have some success when I played. It is wonderful that someone else can now have that success.

Naturally people keep asking me to make comparisons between the two sides, but I have to say that you can't do it because 11 years on it is totally different. What I will say is that I think no matter when Will Carling's England side played they would always do extremely well because they are very good. But comparisons are invidious. I would be temped to say that this year the standard of the opposition has not been that high. Certainly not as good as it was possibly ten or 15 years ago taking Wales as an example, but really it is still a monumentally great achievement. As I have said, to win all four matches takes some doing and this England team did it. Let's not take anything away from them.

Obviously there are differences between the team of 1980 and that of 1991. One of the main ones is that nowadays they are on a training schedule, one that has been carefully worked out and tailored to their individual needs. They are also on a special diet and they have all these tests for fat levels and so on.

We trained hard but we were basically left to our own devices. I was always very confident about the lads around me and trusted them to train hard. There were about eight or nine of us based in the North, including Fran Cotton and Steve Smith, and we used to do extra training sessions during the week.

There was nothing specific about the training I did, I just followed a rule of thumb. It was a case of, 'I'll go out and do some running today'. There was never any question of doing eight 200s or nine 100s or whatever. But I reckon I trained every day when I played. They are obviously a lot more regimented with their preparations. They've got Tom McNab there, dieticians, this, that and the other. It's high-tech training which we certainly didn't have. That was as much through our own ignorance. I admire the amount of time the lads of today put into their game.

But there is something that is common to both teams and that is attitude. When you play for your country you are proud to do so. You want to do well. I know after we played the All Blacks, losing by one point in 1979, I said the side was capable of winning the Championship and I can remember how everybody laughed at me for saying it. But I felt we had the right attitude. We also had what Will's side have had, consistency in selection. We only made the changes forced on us through injury and that helped tremendously.

This England have gone through the international season unchanged for the first time in 30-odd years. And through their manager Geoff Cooke, who is a very good organiser, England have now established a pattern of selection which should guarantee a solid future. That is something we never had.

In my day our numbers were our weakness. There was no real structure for selection. There was no natural progression for players in my day, no way forward. These days, with the league system, there is and our numbers will now become our strength. I feel certain another half-dozen Championships are on the cards this decade. I'm not saying that to put pressure on the players but I think, with the players we can now pick from, England should become one of the strongest sides in the Championship year in, year out even allowing for one of the other sides going well for a time.

There is one other difference between the two Englands. Whereas when I played, the Grand Slam was the pinnacle of your career – apart from going on a British Lions' tour – those lads now have the big one to come – the World Cup. I would love there to have been a World Cup in 1980.

Back then I think England would have stood a good chance of winning it if there had been one. Winning the Grand Slam is wonderful for the supporters and gives them something to shout about as Englishmen, but now there is something else. Once the Grand Slam was over this year people immediately started thinking about England's chances in the World Cup. In 1980 no one had that. Everyone, all the supporters, just sat back and basked in our reflected glory because there was nothing else to do. And I think the players did the same. We settled back for 12 months and savoured the Grand Slam.

This time no one can do that. They can't really afford to do it. The Grand Slam was our Everest. For the team of 1991 it was, in a way, a foothill on the way to their Everest of the World Cup. And they will not even be allowed to relax after the World Cup because, having achieved the Grand Slam and thinking the worst is over on the domestic front, I think they are in for a bit of a shock. They probably feel that the pressure is off and imagine next year it will be less intense. They'll be wrong.

If anything next season will be worse. I speak from experience. The

BILL BEAUMONT, ABLY SUPPORTED BY CURRENT ENGLAND COACH, ROGER UTTLEY, BEARS DOWN ON THE SCOTS, 1980

following year we were under pressure to repeat the feat. The pressure of expectation was intensified. The impression is that having climbed Everest you know the routes so it will be that much easier second time around. But for a start the players, having striven for so long to win everything, then sit back and relax a bit. In a way, perhaps, there is a tendency to think you are slightly better than you really are next time around. Then you lose players through injury, or age or loss of form. The pattern is broken. It is much harder next time. Not many sides have achieved back-to-back Championships in the Five Nations' tournament. You have to ask, having achieved it, are the players then hungry enough for the follow-up? Generally the answer is 'No'. It is not easy to motivate them to repeat it.

However it is not impossible and as I have said I expect England to win half a dozen more titles over the next ten years. Their uncompromising style, which has been criticised, should help.

I feel that their pattern of play this year was determined by their display at Murrayfield last season when Scotland snatched the Grand Slam from them. I think England felt they fell between two stools in 1990. This year I should imagine they thought the only chance opponents would have against them would be from their own mistakes. So Carling and Co. cut out all the errors, played the touchlines, played to their strengths.

The vital guys this year, the men who did as much as anyone to help England win the Grand Slam were Wade Dooley, Paul Ackford, Dean Richards and Hodgkinson. England could afford to play the touchlines because they were very confident – and quite rightly so – that Dooley, Ackford and Richards would win the ball at the line-outs. And when there were any infringements there was Hodgkinson to convert them into points.

In fact, the England pack as a whole has been very much underestimated. I think they are very well organised and confident in their ability to win the ball. And having won it they know their backs will then retain possession. That breeds confidence in the whole side.

The England maul is very much like the New Zealanders'. It is basically a process of bang it up through the middle, then keep driving until eventually you run out of defenders to stop you. One man who has been able to set up the maul for England is Richards. He is the strong man who gives them the platform from which to work. They develop the maul around him. He is so powerful and he is playing so well that he will involve two or three opponents and thus becomes a focal point for the rest of his pack to home in on.

When England and New Zealand meet in the opening match of the World Cup on 3 October at Twickenham it should prove an intriguing confrontation. But not as intriguing as one I would love to have been involved in. A match between this England and my side of 1980.

I'd like to think we'd give them their toughest game to date. Harder than the All Blacks. I know they would give us our toughest game ever. As to who would win? That's easy. England would.

March 1991

GRAND SLAM-WINNING CAPTAIN, BILL BEAUMONT, IS CHAIRED FROM THE FIELD, 1980

Chapter One

WHERE THE JOURNEY BEGAN

By JOHN MASON

NOT EVEN THOSE AT THE EPICENTRE of England's Grand Slam can be certain precisely where the journey began. For some it was round about tea-time at Murrayfield on 17 March 1990, the day that the blooming flowers of Scotland sent the auld enemy homeward tae think again.

Others would vote for a November afternoon in 1988 when England ran Australia ragged at Twickenham in a style that offered handsome hints of all-round qualities sufficient to parade the world stage with honour. Admiring words poured from Bob Dwyer, Australia's coach, in the wake of the 28–19 defeat of the Wallabies.

A smaller contingent, though not needing to thumb through discarded diaries, would settle for the previous autumn on the day that the telephone rang in a Leeds office to determine the answer of a Cumbrian, who had crossed the Pennines in the pursuit of a career in educational administration, to one question. Yes, Geoff Cooke decided, he was willing to become England's team manager and chief coach.

While none of these views would be demonstrably wrong as to where and when the England juggernaut rumbled into gear on the first leg of a fraught expedition labelled Destination Grand Slam, I like to think that the first teetering steps were taken on a damp June Monday afternoon 12,000 miles from home: at Ballymore, Brisbane, the home of Queensland rugby, where they will give considerably more than four x's for failure.

The hoots of derision after England and Wales had presented, arguably, the worst match of the inaugural World Cup in 1987 still ring mockingly. It was quarter-final time and the winners would be pitted against New Zealand, already cast as the probable champions. The radio reporter who thrust a microphone in the face of Mike Harrison, England's captain, was putting a serious question when he asked if the performance of the two teams – Wales won 16–3 – represented the reluctance of the two countries to compete in the World Cup in the first place.

England had conceded two, if not three, soft tries during a miserable contest that did precisely nothing to halt the rapidly tarnishing image of the state of the game in England and Wales. Scotland, in contrast, were being fêted in New Zealand. There was high praise, too, for Irish resilience the previous afternoon against Australia and everywhere they went, the French were being hailed (even in Australia) as the team best able to bring down the All Blacks.

Over a consoling glass that evening Brian Moore, England's hooker, vowed that if international rugby was to continue to play a part in his life, things had to change. There was, he decided, precious little joy in smiling bravely in defeat. To be beaten was bad enough but to subside spinelessly left the taste of bitter aloes.

That World Cup match was Moore's third international. Some 26 caps later, with the tea-cups again rattling on the table, the kettle well and truly on the boil, Moore, deep satisfaction etched in every muddy, tired line on his face, threaded a congratulation-strewn path through a milling, chanting crowd to the Twickenham dressing-rooms, the Grand Slam won.

The clock said 4.14 p.m. on Saturday, 16 March 1991 – and it was not raining, it was pouring. 'We're not failures any more,' were Moore's first words as he reached the comparative haven of the tunnel beneath the cavernous, echoing West Stand.

With all the implications still to percolate a weary body and mind, Moore,

ENGLAND GRAND SLAM TEAM MANAGER, GEOFF COOKE

BRIAN MOORE: 'WE'RE NOT FAILURES ANY MORE'

who shared in the 1989 British Lions Test-winning series in Australia, cannot be sure whether what he said was a spontaneous reaction to four years' hard labour or the instinctive answer to the first of a myriad of questions. The fear of failure had been erased.

Four of Moore's colleagues on that June afternoon at Ballymore four years previously were mighty pillars of mutual support at damp Twickenham – Wade Dooley, Peter Winterbottom, Dean Richards and Rory Underwood. Jeff Probyn, the Grand Slam tighthead, was also in Brisbane, so it transpired, as a non-playing reserve.

Jonathan Webb and Paul Rendall were on both team sheets – as players in the first England-Wales match to be played overseas, and as bench reserves against the French three years, nine months and eight days later. Mick Skinner was involved, too, as a reserve on both occasions.

All, some more actively than others, had been required to be in attendance for one of the definitive Five Nations' Championship matches of all time, a marvellous sporting occasion which had ended in victory for England by 21 points to 19: the culmination of a great deal of sweat, not a little blood and, here and there, even a few tears. I always knew these hulks were sentimental softies at heart.

The seeds of declarations made with spirits at the lowest of ebbs had borne fruit. More pertinently still, as Probyn insisted that evening in the ornate surrounds of the Hilton Hotel at the post-match dinner, England's rugby players had reminded the world that, contrary to popular belief, they could win the pressure matches.

Pressure. The exertion of continuous force – the force so exerted, upon or against a body by another in contact with it. The dictionary definition mirrors the performance of England's pack, their most potent weapon of the Grand Slam campaign. Probyn, though, was not in that instance making that particular point. His reference was to pressure as in a high degree of activity and speed, of varying tensions or constraining influences, of the desire to succeed or, deep, deep down, I suppose, the need not to fail. Everything has a history and in the case of England's top rugby players, it was not necessary to be close to them to know how much the events of 17 March 1990, at Murrayfield, hurt – and still do.

Roger Uttley, a granite boulder of reliability who has the unique distinction of playing in England's previous Grand Slam side and, 11 years later, coaching the next, said bravely in assessment of the 1991 performance that defeat the previous year in Edinburgh had been no bad thing. Such cool rationalisation sounds good but it takes time because that was not the reaction when Scotland marched away with (1) the Grand Slam, (2) the Five Nations' Championship, (3) the Triple Crown and (4) the Calcutta Cup. Not a bad haul for the scavengers, said Scotland's management in a mocking reference to an out-of-context comment made the previous season by Geoff Cooke, England's manager. Scotland were not amused.

DEAN RICHARDS
PRESSURES AUSTRALIA, 1988

GILBER

What Uttley had in mind when he spoke at an RFU briefing at Twickenham on the Monday after victory over France was the psychological importance of the 1991 championship season in relation to the World Cup in the autumn. Winning titles was about peaks of performance. The intense difficulties inherent in sustaining standards, the dangers of reaching optimum levels too early, would have been a further burden of expectation.

The irony of the mental gymnastics involved in turning the crushing disappointment of the 1990 defeat into a virtue was not lost on a mostly cynical media audience. Nor, for that matter, do I doubt that the coach, a 1974 British Lion and a former England captain, had too many false illusions.

Roger Uttley is the epitome of the person you would want at your back on jungle patrol: the craggy, salt of the earth type whose part in England's three years of mounting success cannot be exaggerated. He is intent on retiring from his honorary post following the World Cup after spending 18 of the past 21 years or so in the service of English rugby at the sharp end. The national debt – to Uttley, that is – is enormous.

The honours list, though, must not be restricted to selected individuals, Dean Richards, the most modest star of them, apart. In declaring a sneaking regard for Sam Goldwyn, who once ordered his script-writers to think up some new clichés, I believe the single other factor in England's Grand Slam was teamwork.

It is too simplistic to say that Simon Hodgkinson won the Championship because he kicked a record 60 points or that Rory Underwood's try eight minutes from time in Dublin settled the issue. Both, of course, had major contributions to make and without them, the machine might have stuttered to an untimely halt.

By the same token, though, the precise tactical kicking of outside-half Rob Andrew, the most improved player in international rugby worldwide, and the electric pass of Richard Hill from the base of the scrum kept the momentum rolling. They, too, were expert in sustaining the pressure – that word again – on fallible opponents.

Yet all of them, the off-the-field support team of reserves, management and RFU staff included, would have failed without the fuel to power that machinery: the five-star, or should it be eight, gallons supplied endlessly by the pack. It is time to salute Jason Leonard, Brian Moore, Jeff Probyn, Paul Ackford, Wade Dooley, Mike Teague, Peter Winterbottom and Dean Richards, a happy mix of seasoned warriors who have soldiered in common cause and mutual respect. When the going got tough, they got tougher. Without them, the wheels would not only have come off; the juggernaut would not have started. The journey would not have begun.

The post-mortems would have been endless and the friendly substantial ghost of Bill Beaumont, the captain of the 1980 side, would have continued to stalk the English stage. Cheerful, matter-of-fact person that he is, Beaumont was among the first to congratulate the class of '91. He was BBC TV's match summariser for the Grand Slam decider and not even implacable Bill could keep fluttering frissons of fright out of his voice when France got back to 21–19 with about three minutes, allowing for injuries, remaining.

Should that comment be misconstrued in any way, the man from *The Independent* will willingly tell the world that *The Daily Telegraph*'s chief rugby writer was bawling at considerable decibels when Underwood set off on his run in Dublin. Apparently when England's record try-scorer decided to take on (and beat) Keith Crossan, I was imploring him to pass to Hodgkinson, who had stayed on course on the outside after their scissors moments before.

Say it myself, I have been renowned for watching matches in silence, probably because during highly enjoyable days of apprenticeship as an evening paper reporter in Bristol, we kept an open line to the office and I did not dare upset Mrs Roberts, my copy-taker, by continually shouting exhortations to errant Bristol forwards in her ears.

Did I mention, by the way, that *The Independent*'s chief rugby wallah had opted for Paris (France v Wales), not rainy, fraught Dublin where England were very nearly bunkered? Well, the Indo did send their golf writer, whose other claim to fame is that he was at school with Clive Norling. I digress . . .

After falling at the final hurdle the previous March, England did not distinguish themselves either on the seven-match trip to Argentina in July. It was a full-scale tour, complete with two internationals, but without a three-line whip for the senior players, all but one of whom had been involved in the 1989 Lions Test-winning series in Australia.

Of the forwards it was time, said management, for Ackford, Teague and Richards to rest. Andrew, Guscott and Underwood, who missed the chance of touring with his youngest brother, Tony, were also told to put their feet up. Quite what the Argentines thought of receiving a semi-second string side labelled England, no one dared ask.

The Pumas were splendid hosts – off the field – and though going down in the first international, they came from behind to win the second. Delighted as they were, few of the more astute local observers attached great credence to the victory, not even Rudolfo O'Reilly, the volatile Argentine coach who, for the second time, retired after the series.

Hodgkinson, Carling and Hill were present to assist England's younger players in their quest for caps. So, too, was Oti, who surprised all and sundry (himself, too, probably) by playing more matches than anyone and coming through unscathed. The senior forwards required to gallop about the pampas were Moore, Probyn, Dooley and Winterbottom, so that in a first-choice team unaffected by injury, England had a nucleus of seven of what was to become the Grand Slam team.

Two more were on hand, though neither was counting chickens, or anything else, come to that – Leonard, the loosehead, and wing three-quarter Nigel Heslop, the Merseyside policeman, who had attracted admiring attention on a Services-Police tour of New Zealand in 1988. As Paul Rendall, the omnipotent Hanging Judge of the Players' Court, had been left behind in sunny Slough devising devious deprivations for the selectors, Leonard, who was barely 21, had only Victor Ubogu between him and his first cap. Leonard, the self-employed carpenter from Barking, won hands down but, in the true traditions of the Front-Row Union, diplomatically insisted that The Judge, and Ubogu, were not through yet.

Heslop, 27, had a similarly trouble-free run as the challenge from Tony Underwood was muted, not only on fitness grounds. Several seasons of club rugby with Liverpool, Waterloo and Orrell and representative duties with Lancashire, the North and British Police had given Heslop's play a robust cutting edge. He, too, came back with two caps and his first international try.

So the Pumas, later to be savaged at Twickenham in November when Hugo Porta, recalled as captain and outside half at 39, tried manfully to keep advancing years at bay, were confronted in Buenos Aires at the Velez Sarsfield Stadium by nine of what would become the 1991 Grand Slam team. As England, including non-internationals, won only one of four matches at this soccer ground in the outer suburbs of that sprawling, vibrant city, thoughts of the UK domestic programme ahead were fondly considered. They knew that the return of Ackford, Richards, Andrew, Guscott and Rory Underwood would get the show back on the road.

Effectively there were three places in serious contention: loosehead (Rendall/Leonard), flanker (Teague/Skinner/Hall), right wing (Rory Underwood/Heslop), assuming, unwisely possibly, that Oti would be fit to play on the left. Contingencies for injuries were talked about rather in the manner of condemning anti-social behaviour – necessary but not nice. In the event Oti, a 1989 touring Lion, was hurt in a Sevens training session in September and the contest for right wing never really started. Heslop required no second bidding and with Rory Underwood well pleased to reappear unchallenged on the left, things worked out well for everyone except the unfortunate Oti.

At a time when top-level rugby union relies heavily upon the generosity of employers to make individuals available, it was a bitter twist that Oti, who did not play again for five months, should have been hurt on a Sunday afternoon while preparing for an event in which his company of chartered surveyors and property agents had a leading role. He had been training with England in the morning.

The replacements' bench was a hive of intense industry and speculation, too. Of the squad that went to Argentina, it was plain that John Olver, late of Harlequins and valuable recruit at Northampton, and Mick Skinner, the joker in the pack, would be burrowing into their track-suits.

Indeed, Olver, who led Harlequins for three years and is an acknowledged Sevens expert, having started rugby life as a flanker, declares that in his

ROGER UTTLEY, 'THE EPITOME OF THE PERSON YOU WOULD WANT AT YOUR BACK ON JUNGLE PATROL'

MERSEYSIDE POLICEMAN NIGEL HESLOP KEEPS HIS EYE ON THE BALL AS RICHARD HILL BACKS UP

capacity as a reserve hooker at more levels than he cares to remember, he has watched more matches than any member of the press corps. He has certainly talked as much, that is for sure.

Dewi Morris, the try-scoring scrum half who switched in the summer from Liverpool St Helens to Orrell, was also a cast-iron candidate for the bench. Like the other two, his rollicking good humour is a quality that endears him to colleagues and selectors alike. Who, for goodness sake, in English ranks would have known the words (or the key) of that Welsh signature tune anyway?

Selection of replacements is also a mildly tricky business in that once the specialist positions of hooker and scrum half have been looked after, the competent all-rounder, who might not necessarily win promotion if there were a pre-match injury, comes into his own. John Buckton, who won two more caps on tour, got first refusal, as it were, as reserve centre. There was a recall, too, for the hugely competent Gary Rees, the first of whose caps was in South Africa in 1984. He collected another cap in that astonishing afternoon against Argentina at Twickenham on 3 November when England ran in seven tries in a 51–0 tousing of the proud Pumas. Webb, England's World Cup fullback in 1987, had completed his rehabilitation sufficiently well with Bath, having left Bristol, that he was reserve to Hodgkinson. Leonard had won the loosehead spot, so Rendall was on the bench and, seeking a few sparks to ignite a weary Moore, the selectors decided that he and Olver should change places, the latter winning his first cap.

All of that, though, was nothing more than an interesting run-down on the rankings at that time. The fluttering in the dovecotes concerned the return of John Hall, the Bath flanker, after three years out of contention for a variety of reasons, some of his own volition.

Hall celebrated recall with one of the seven tries and, with Rees back in the frame as reserve, England could discard from strength. There was no room for Skinner and the word on Teague, who had not been in Argentina, was that, besides being sorely troubled by a recurring shoulder injury, the legacy of his work for the Lions in 1989, he was not playing well in his club position of number eight for Gloucester. He was the talk of the steamie – which, my dear Glaswegian wife tells me, is Scottish for the communal laundry room.

Could it be that Teague, voted Player of the Series in Australia in 1989, was about to be shunted off to the sidings to see out his rugby days as remaindered rolling stock? Having hinted at such a possibility – unless there was a total return to form – in a *Daily Telegraph* piece in mid-November as the ADT Divisional Championship loomed into sight, phone and post-bag buckled under the strain of indignant protest. Teague, I am happy to record, merely smiled. He was keeping his powder dry.

Nor did that mean that all bets had been switched to Hall, at least not as far as he was concerned. In a gentle rebuke Hall suggested when we next met that I had been a little grudging in my account of his activities in the Argentina match. In case I failed to convince him that that was not my intention, we have a modest wager that he will be in the World Cup first-choice team. If not, I pay him.

But well as Hall, in his first international for three-and-a-half years, played against Porta & Company, there were alarm bells ringing, too. The grapevine whisper was that Hall was 'carrying a knee', which is rugbyspeak for ligament or cartilage problems or worse.

John Taylor, a flank forward who put in the odd performance or three, expressed a kindly professional interest at the next Bath match as well as in his journalistic capacity of guarding deadlines, as opposed to try-lines. Hall told the *Mail on Sunday* that everything would be fine and that he was resting as a precaution. If Hall's fingers were not crossed at the time, they should have been because, alas, he was wrong. He got to Lanzarote for the New Year training camp but, as he had done four years previously in Sydney, Hall could not complete the prolonged sessions.

Back came a slimmed-down Teague, who had played for England against the centenary-celebrating Barbarians and for them against Wales in the opening weeks of the season. Any queries as to his fitness had evaporated in the sunshine land of the Canaries.

It is possible these days to quantify physical fitness mathematically. The figures removed all reservations prompted by previously doubting eyes: Teague was the fittest player in the squad. The stamina and speed tests said so, so did the recovery rates – yet another example of the meticulous preparation that has become England's badge of honour.

Having lasted approximately three seconds on his last England appearance at Cardiff in 1989 when felled directly after the kick-off ('I gave them hell while I was on'), Teague, who had been working on the weights, was well pleased to be back. He had, he reckoned, more than 79 minutes unfinished business to complete.

Selection was hardly a problem, not that management were unduly anxious to say so publicly. Of the team who eased past the Barbarians 18–16 ('No Tea-Party at Twickers', said *Rugby World*) on 29 September in a fairly serious contest despite the occasion, 14 were in the England side seeking a first victory at Cardiff for 28 years. The exception was Moore and it was no surprise when he reclaimed the hooking duties ahead of the loyal Olver. On the bench Buckton, the Saracens captain, who had received a nasty scalp wound the previous Saturday in a league match with Wasps, was replaced by the London and Wasps rising star, Damian Hopley, a 20-year-old centre built in the style of a large brick outhouse. He had not been on the senior national bench before.

England's whistling in the dark began early. 'The burden of expectation' swiftly became an overworked phrase and there was an edginess within the ranks that those of us who knew them well could understand, without signalling approval.

In the Mason family we pretended we knew all would be well. It had been my birthday on 29 September and England won. It was my mother's 80th birthday on 19 January, match day, and she assured me that a gift-wrapped victory was a foregone conclusion. She would be deserting her afternoon guests to watch the match on television. I chose not to remind her that the previous win, 28 years ago, had also been on 19 January.

At Gloucester, where the team assembled, a first England request that I can recollect for a training session 'in private' was respected. When Geoff Cooke disclosed that tapes of *Hen Wlad fy Nhadau*, the anthem of Wales, were being played incessantly on the team coach, the journalists happily forgave the management. Here were food and drink for all scribblers (and cartoonists), no matter the style of their publication.

That was the last light-hearted moment for about 72 hours. Senior RFU officials dismissed rumours that England's players were seeking a showdown about the lack of consistency, country to country, of International Board regulations governing amateurism and, so they claimed, of a dragging of feet by the RFU. The match squad withdrew, as best they could, from public gaze.

The match was a welcome relief, in many respects, doubly so in retrospect. A mostly unsuspecting media had settled uncomfortably into the Arms Park press box, obituaries for Welsh rugby at the ready. Those of us of the English contingent were desperately trying not to smirk, not visibly anyway. Having been present on 19 January 1963, when my pen belonged to the *Bristol Evening Post* and my voice to BBC West Region, the 28 intervening years slipped effortlessly away. Hodgkinson's seven penalty goals (a record) and a late try by the masterful Teague swept England to the largest win in Cardiff.

Yet such competence was also an anti-climax. When pride, dignity and sportsmanship should have been jostling for position, England, despite a satisfying victory, spoilt it. They declined to be interviewed by television or newspapers, apparently because they wanted a fee of £5,000 payable to the marketing company they had formed. The BBC, having informed the RFU, said 'No' and, though there was no personal quarrel with the hardy perennials of the rugby press, the block went on us, too. Not all was sweetness and light and, pursued by an irate press pack, there was the unedifying business of England players leaving by the hotel's kitchens and Cooke, England's besieged manager, calling for hotel security to remove reporters lurking in the corridor outside his room.

Somehow the match-winning formula which called for unyielding control up front, slide-rule kicking for position and an ice-cool Hodgkinson to tighten any remaining screws took second place. Though apologies quickly followed, beginning when by chance I gained an exclusive interview with Will Carling, England's captain, the next afternoon in Gloucester, media relations in a sport which had prided itself on its easy-going tolerance had been sorely damaged.

In playing matters, the grumbles and gripes about unambitious England

MIKE TEAGUE PROVIDES HIS OWN VERSION OF 'ROLLING STOCK'

TEAGUE AND DOOLEY: 'WE WANT THEM'

were far less acceptable. I wrote in *The Daily Telegraph* that Monday: 'For as long as England go on winning, the need to broaden their attacking scope, to alter the script of what they seek to do, would be academic. Why fiddle with the body trim when the efficient engine has ample power in reserve?'

Weeks later, mission accomplished, England's steely efficient players had every right to feel ill-used by some critics, the most vociferous of whom possessed Antipodean accents. Surely Griz Wyllie, the All Blacks coach, cannot be that worried – can he? Nor, though I write six months in advance, do I believe that England, despite the 1991 Grand Slam, Five Nations' title, Triple Crown and Calcutta Cup plus 12 wins in a run of 14 internationals, will prevail in the World Cup. As a patriot, though, I would dearly like to have those last few words rammed down my throat round about 4.30 p.m. on Saturday, 3 November 1991.

The bitter-sweet memories of Cardiff plagued England for a month because they were not involved in the next batch of Five Nations' matches a fortnight later. Again the ghosts of seasons past haunted Carling and his colleagues. By now, though, they had listened to the advice of media friends and if the PR bit was not always the smoothest of exercises, no one could possibly accuse England's spokesmen of arrogance. Respect for their opponents decorated every public utterance.

As Scotland, the defending champions, were the visitors to Twickenham, the Save & Prosper international on 16 February 1991 had an added piquancy or, as Wade Dooley told me so succinctly in a *Daily Telegraph* interview, 'We want them.' Scotland, undone by the massive competence of England's pack and a certain D. Richards, who had been absent the previous year at Murrayfield, duly departed empty-handed. They left behind (graciously) a clutch of 1990 titles in the safe keeping of long-term rivals – and friends. Should that latter contention be doubted, ask Finlay Calder how he regards Brian Moore. Quiz Richards about his respect for John Jeffrey. Get any England forward to talk about Chris Gray. Hear Scott Hastings on . . . anyone.

Next stop: Dublin, in the rain. Hodgkinson on 38 points (21 against Wales, 17 against Scotland) and only seven required to remove Dusty Hare's English record of 44 in a Five Nations' season from the lists. He succeeded, yet, amid gasps of relief or disbelief depending on your fancy, missed his first three kicks at goal.

But as England's fullback, as he had done when the admirable Heslop scored against Scotland, also had a delicate hand in the try that secured the Triple Crown, there was ample to celebrate. He worked a perfect scissors with Underwood, which provided the essential space the wing required for arguably the most important of his 27 international tries. England's sweet chariot was swinging high, not low.

Ostentation, though, is not Hodgkinson's style. He hides away as best he can in the drawn out preliminaries to an international, deep in his own

ENGLAND FLANKER MIKE TEAGUE CHARGES AT THE WELSH DEFENCE, JANUARY 1991.

TEAGUE DIVES OVER FOR THE TRY AGAINST WALES. DOOLEY HELPS OUT AND MOORE CELEBRATES, JANUARY 1991.

DOOLEY AND RICHARDS TRACK THE BALL, WATCHED BY PAUL ARNOLD OF WALES, JANUARY 1991.

ROGER UTTLEY, THE ENGLAND COACH, PUNCHES HOME A POINT ON THE TACKLE BAG.

MIKE TEAGUE, JEFF PROBYN, BRIAN MOORE AND JASON LEONARD PREPARE TO SCRUM DOWN AGAINST THE SCOTS, FEBRUARY 1991.

DAVID SOLE OF SCOTLAND IS TACKLED BY WADE DOOLEY AND MIKE TEAGUE, FEBRUARY 1991.

PAUL ACKFORD WINS A LINE-OUT FOR ENGLAND AGAINST THE SCOTS, FEBRUARY 1991.

NIGEL HESLOP TOUCHES DOWN FOR ENGLAND AGAINST SCOTLAND, FEBRUARY 1991.

MIKE TEAGUE FEEDS THE BALL BACK FOR ENGLAND AGAINST IRELAND, MARCH 1991.

SIMON GEOGHEGAN SCORES IRELAND'S ONLY TRY AGAINST ENGLAND, MARCH 1991.

RORY UNDERWOOD SCORES THE FIRST OF ENGLAND'S TWO TRIES AGAINST IRELAND, MARCH 1991.

ROB ANDREW IN ACTION AGAINST THE IRISH, MARCH 1991.

MIKE TEAGUE DIVES OVER THE IRISH LINE TO SCORE ENGLAND'S SECOND TRY, MARCH 1991.

thoughts, willing himself to concentrate, flicking through mental pictures of the ball sailing high between the posts. While not denigrating the value of such thought processes, I would venture that supreme technique is as important – that plus, as Alan Davies, the Nottingham coach who taught him as a teenager, insisted in a telegram to him before the France match, the need to relax.

Dublin was tough. With barely eight minutes remaining, little of that forward pressure had borne fruit. Matthews had a marvellous match for Ireland and though Rigney, Francis and Robinson could not exceed the heavyweight skills of Ackford, Dooley and Richards, fire and brimstone had apprehensive Englishmen back on their heels.

Underwood altered that when leaving three, if not four, Irishmen scrabbling at thin air as they sought to tackle. Underwood even had the audacity to ignore Hodgkinson, who had stayed in easy reach at his left shoulder. Teague tidied up with a second try, thanks to Andrew, Leonard and Richards, and the conversion from touch took Hodgkinson to 46 points and the Grand Slam decider to come.

The Twickenham stage presented a theatrical spectacle that afternoon, the like of which in a match of this importance had rarely, if ever, been seen there previously. Billy Williams's cabbage patch was transformed into an ornate tableau, albeit a damp one, that illustrated most of the virtues of the best team game I know.

The sequence of giddy events, expertly refereed by Les Peard, is chronicled fully elsewhere. Suffice here that England's forwards again reduced the opposition to a spent force: Ackford ruled the front of the line-out and the mobile maul denied Blanco and Sella and Mesnel and Saint-André all but a sniff of the ball. That was still sufficient for France to score three tries to one and at 21–19 England were thankful that the journey begun in hope practically four years earlier was within seconds of ending – in triumph. It was raining, too.

Chapter Two

FROM GOSFORTH TO TWICKENHAM

By BARRIE FAIRALL

ENGLAND'S BUILD-UP began in northern climes at the wonderfully appointed Kingston Park, a Sunday afternoon celebration last September of the Gosforth club's change of name and new ground, the English players rounding off their training weekend with a 32–6 victory over the side now referred to as Newcastle Gosforth.

Fielding eight members of the previous season's Five Nations' team, another four who had toured Argentina during the summer, the returning Dean Richards and two newcomers, this English selection were never likely to be troubled by a team who five months previously had the misfortune to finish bottom of the Second Division, a status they were to maintain owing to the fact that there was no relegation.

While Newcastle Gosforth had to be content with their two penalties from Graham Spearman, the English XV were to run in seven tries. 'The game,' Geoff Cooke, the manager, said afterwards, 'fulfilled its purpose as useful practice.' Richards, meanwhile, convinced those present that he was rapidly returning to full fitness and was one of the team's four try-scorers prior to the interval.

The crashing progress to the line by Richards had been instigated by a line-out tap from Paul Ackford, who had been first to breach the host club's defence. Chris Oti (two), Alan Buzza, the young lock Steve Shortland and Rory Underwood completed the English try count, Rob Andrew adding to the scoreline with a couple of conversions.

The stroll completed, England's next outing at the end of the month took them to headquarters for a meeting with the centenary-celebrating Barbarians. 'These occasions,' wrote Stephen Jones in *The Sunday Times*, 'are always in danger of becoming candyfloss affairs, with try after try to gladden the eye but no real confrontation to bring a deeper satisfaction. Yet the sense of fulfilment at the end of a thumping contest was undeniable . . . Lovers of candyfloss would have been taken aback by the opening exchanges. Campese was tackled thunderously hard three times inside 20 seconds. There was real bite in the tackling and the likes of Loe and Rush of the Barbarians and Dooley and Richards of England played as if their lives depended on it.'

In his report for *The Independent on Sunday*, Chris Rea said: 'There is a story, perhaps as old as the Barbarians themselves, but one much beloved of rugby folk, about a tribe of Lilliputians condemned to living in tall grass whose plaintive and invariably blasphemous cries could be heard demanding to know where they were. And so it was, during the third quarter of this exciting and always entertaining game, that rugby's most exclusive black band of nomadic tribesmen lost their way in Twickenham's excessively long blades.'

Yes, in front of a 50,000 crowd, England were to win through – but only with two points to spare at 18–16 and after the prolific Wallaby Michael Lynagh had missed relatively easy kicks at goal. Simon Hodgkinson, meanwhile, made a 14-point contribution to the England cause by scoring a try and landing two conversions and two penalties. Richards, driven over in the corner, claimed the other English try.

If the Barbarians had tested England's playing ability, the arrival of Argentina at Twickenham early in November was to provide a test of temperament. While a scoreline reading 51–0 was a crushing revenge for the summer's Test reversal in Buenos Aires, it was the crushing blow delivered by Federico Mendez, the teenage Puma prop, on Ackford that caused the lasting ripples. While a wobbling Ackford was helped off, Mendez was sent off at the insistence of Ken McCartney, the Scot who was officiating as a touch judge.

Writing of Mendez's punishment in *The Independent*, Steve Bale said: 'The ludicrously lenient four-week suspension – enough to make last season's international culprits, Kevin Moseley and Alain Carminati, choke – was accompanied by complaints of provocation which explained Mendez's irrationality but in no way excused an assault on a wholly innocent party which could have done Ackford permanent damage. Moseley and Carminati received seven-month sentences; Mendez, a tearful schoolboy with a big future in this man's world, got off lightly.'

And the affair was by no means over. While England had registered seven tries, Underwood's hat-trick extending his England record to 25 and Hodgkinson kicking 23 points to break Dan Lambert's 79-year-old England record for a match, Jeff Probyn was to undergo a trial by video. Probyn came into the frame, or rather freeze-frame, when the Rugby Football Union was asked to study a recording of events leading up to the punch of the season. The Pumas claimed that Mendez had been provoked and the Four Home Unions' committee that had banned him ordered the RFU to carry out an investigation. The trial, though, was to backfire because Mendez was seen punching and then clutching Probyn's groin before the England prop was

FEDERICO MENDEZ RECEIVES HIS MARCHING ORDERS FROM REFEREE HAWKE IN ENGLAND'S 51–0 VICTORY OVER ARGENTINA, 1990

pictured standing on his adversary. Indeed, it looked as if the youngster was let off far too lightly after being involved in not one, but two unsavoury incidents. Sympathy for Probyn was then reflected in an RFU statement. 'The panel of inquiry was unanimously of the opinion that Probyn had not committed an offence which merited further action. Slow-motion clearly showed that Probyn endeavoured to avoid the fallen Argentinian by stepping over him. Probyn was then attacked twice by Mendez from his position on the ground and Mendez still had hold of his groin at the moment when Probyn trod on him in an effort to make him release his grip.' The RFU also registered concern about the risk of wrong conclusions being drawn from televised pictures.

Probyn thus flew off to Bermuda for a rugby jolly, happy in the knowledge that he was not going to be punished for reacting to having his shorts felt. His next trip, mind, was of a rather more serious nature, England jetting off in January for their annual squad training in Lanzarote. And such was the ferocity of England's work that the selectors had no option but to delay the announcement of the team due to tackle the Welsh in Cardiff. Two match practice sessions resulted in the Bath flanker John Hall damaging a medial ligament in his right knee and the Harlequins hooker Brian Moore suffering a neck injury. Sadly for Hall, who had marked his England comeback with a try against Argentina, the injury came too late for him to win a place in the Five Nations' battles to come.

Chapter Three

THE MATCH REPORTS

By JOHN MASON

19 January, Cardiff Arms Park

TEDIUM TAKES THE EDGE OFF BANISHMENT OF WELSH GHOST

Wales 6
England 25

THE DAY OF RECKONING in Cardiff was such a long time coming that its arrival after 28 years bordered on anti-climax. Victory over Wales by such a margin should have been a joyous occasion on which pride, dignity and sportsmanship jostled for position.

Yet even without the mealy-mouthed refusal of management and players to talk about England's first win at the Arms Park since 1963, the match did little to quicken the pulse.

Victory by a try and seven penalty goals to two penalty goals was a solid achievement based on immaculate goal-kicking by Simon Hodgkinson, the superiority of England's forwards and the gritty resourcefulness of scrum half Richard Hill.

Across the board, the performance was workmanlike, which is rugbyspeak for tedious fare that, the winning and the laying of ghosts apart, does precisely nothing to increase the universal appeal of the game.

If international rugby players, as has been claimed, want to be paid for their co-operation, they have moved the goalposts – the game at the top

WALES 6	ENGLAND 25
P. H. Thorburn (*Neath*) captain	S. D. Hodgkinson (*Nottingham*)
I. C. Evans (*Llanelli*) M. G. Ring (*Cardiff*)	N. J. Heslop (*Orrell*) W. D. C. Carling (*Harlequins*) captain
I. S. Gibbs (*Neath*) S. P. Ford (*Cardiff*)	J. C. Guscott (*Bath*) R. Underwood (*Leicester & RAF*)
N. R. Jenkins (*Pontypridd*) R. N. Jones (*Swansea*)	C. R. Andrew (*Wasps*) R. J. Hill (*Bath*)
B. R. Williams (*Swansea*) K. H. Phillips (*Neath*) P. Knight (*Pontypridd*)	J. Leonard (*Harlequins*) B. C. Moore (*Harlequins*) J. A. Probyn (*Wasps*)
G. D. Llewellyn (*Pontypridd*) G. O. Llewellyn (*Neath*)	P. J. Ackford (*Harlequins*) W. A. Dooley (*Preston Grasshoppers*)
G. M. George (*Neath*) A J. Carter (*Newport*) P. Arnold (*Swansea*)	M. C. Teague (*Gloucester*) P. J. Winterbottom (*Harlequins*) D. Richards (*Leicester*)
Replacement: C. J. Bridges (*Neath*) for Jones (49 minutes)	
	Try: Teague
Penalty goals: Thorburn, Jenkins	**Penalty goals:** Hodgkinson (7)

Referee: R. J. Megson (Scotland)

DEAN RICHARDS ATTACKS THE WELSH

end no longer remains the skilled exercise of amateurs at play: it becomes a branch of the entertainment business.

On that score, even allowing for the cool precision of the seemingly frail Hodgkinson, the massive contributions in every sense of the locks, Ackford and Dooley, plus Teague, the try-scorer, England's efforts were about as exciting as watching the tide turn in Swansea Bay.

England's players have said that they prefer to do their talking on the field and that with a month to go before they meet Scotland in the Calcutta Cup at Twickenham, they want to sit back and relax. The events of Saturday have left them 'emotionally drained'.

For as long as England go on winning, the need to broaden their attacking scope, to alter the script of what they seek to do, would be academic. Why fiddle with the body trim when the efficient engine has ample power in reserve?

Plainly the match-winning formula of Saturday will be the firm base for a campaign which, with home matches against Scotland and France, should net the three titles on offer – the Triple Crown, the Championship and the Grand Slam.

Against Wales, whose scrum did not disintegrate as had been widely expected, England could still afford to coast at times. Wales, helped hugely by Robert Jones, the scrum-half, were primarily engaged in a damage-limiting operation and while shutting England down at various points of strength, they could not dictate.

Thorburn, the Welsh saviour on so many occasions and his country's leading points-scorer, began with a penalty goal in the second minute when England were offside.

The frantic fervour of the singing in appreciation of these points did not last. In the fifth minute, Hodgkinson stepped forward to kick his first goal after a scrum had been collapsed and in the 13th he put England ahead, never to be caught.

Further penalty goals from Hodgkinson followed in the 21st, 25th, 50th, 54th and 69th minutes to complete a new entry among the world records for penalty goals by an individual in an international. How idiotic of his colleagues – and his manager and coach – not to allow him to talk about his feat afterwards.

It was a pity, too, that Thorburn, who anxiously sought responsibility for not having increased the pressures on England, missed kicks two, three, four and five at goal. Only one of those penalty attempts was not comfortably within his customary range.

All were in the first half and though ifs and ands do not win matches, instead of being 12–3 adrift at the break, Wales could have been only 12–9 down, even 12–12. How England would have responded must be a debating point only.

Thorburn, the captain, was sufficiently annoyed with himself that he asked

Neil Jenkins, the new outside-half, to kick for goal in the sixth minute of the second half. Jenkins obliged from 30 metres out on the right following an English line-out offence and again the singing, this time echoing relief, briefly raised the roof.

Four minutes later Hodgkinson put over penalty goal number six and Wales were confronted with the impossible task, at this stage of their rebuilding, of needing to score three times to win.

England's try had its roots in a chip deep to the right-hand corner by Hill. Ford did well to prevent the try then and there, and from the scrum the back row finally removed that millstone around English necks.

Richards, who by his tremendous standards had a curate's egg of a match, picked up. Teague was at his shoulder and as the wedge erupted from the second row to drive him on, the flanker grounded the ball.

Hodgkinson could not convert but with the eagle-eyed referee, Ray Megson, exerting shrewd control, England's seventh penalty goal pulled down the curtain on what had been the longest-running saga in the rugby business.

16 February, Twickenham

EDGE OF STEEL CUTS PATH TO PRIZE CROWN FOR ENGLAND

England 21
Scotland 12

ENGLAND'S COMPETENCE and nuts-and-bolts efficiency, which prevents the opposition from imposing their will, should be sufficient to earn them most, if not all, of the prizes this season. The World Cup, though, is another matter.

The latest unflurried exercise of basic skills, teamwork and goal-kicking of the highest order sent Scotland, having relinquished the Calcutta Cup, empty-handed from Twickenham in more ways than one on Saturday. Whatever Scotland managed, England did that little better in the Save & Prosper international.

Victory by a goal and five penalty goals to four penalty goals left England, who play Ireland in Dublin on Saturday week, on reasonably comfortable course for the Triple Crown – not that the team's spokesmen were making anything remotely resembling such a claim after dispatching the Scots.

That France, who first meet Wales in Paris in a fortnight, will be at Twickenham in a month's time with probably the season's prime honours at stake, was barely mentioned. The one-match-at-a-time syndrome was eagerly embraced, so great was England's desire not to be labelled arrogant.

There is a finely tempered edge of steel in this side, the unyielding spine of which ensures that the opposition, starved of possession, have to make do and mend.

Locks, number eight, outside half and fullback are the team within the team, the command centre able in their varying capacities to pin the opposition down: Ackford and Dooley at line-out and scrum, Teague at close quarters, Richards everywhere, Andrew with the precision of his tactical kicking and Hodgkinson with practically everything else.

On Saturday, if a screw needed to be turned a fraction more, Hodgkinson, stroking the ball with the finesse of the better cover-drives in which power is well-nigh incidental, modestly obliged. He was also perfectly positioned to provide the scoring pass for Heslop's try, adding a masterly conversion.

Having kicked penalty goals in the 14th, 17th and 34th minutes,

ENGLAND 21

S. D. Hodgkinson (*Nottingham*)

N. J. Heslop (*Orrell*)
W. D. C. Carling (*Harlequins*) captain
J. C. Guscott (*Bath*)
R. Underwood (*Leicester & RAF*)

C. R. Andrew (*Wasps*)
R. J. Hill (*Bath*)

J. Leonard (*Harlequins*)

B. C. Moore (*Harlequins*)
J. A. Probyn (*Wasps*)

P. J. Ackford (*Harlequins*)
W. A. Dooley (*Preston Grasshoppers*)

M. C. Teague (*Gloucester*)
P. J. Winterbottom (*Harlequins*)
D. Richards (*Leicester*)

Try: Heslop

Conversion: Hodgkinson

Penalty goals: Hodgkinson (5)

SCOTLAND 12

A. G. Hastings (*Watsonians*)

A. G. Stanger (*Hawick*)
S. Hastings (*Watsonians*)

S. R. P. Lineen (*Boroughmuir*)
A. Moore (*Edinburgh Academicals*)

C. M. Chalmers (*Melrose*)
G. Armstrong (*Jedforest*)

D. M. B. Sole (*Edinburgh Academicals*) captain
K. S. Milne (*Heriot's FP*)
A. P. Burnell (*London Scottish*)

C. A. Gray (*Nottingham*)
D. F. Cronin (*Bath*)

D. J. Turnbull (*Hawick*)
J. Jeffrey (*Kelso*)
D. B. White (*London Scottish*)

Penalty goals: Chalmers (4)

Referee: S. R. Hilditch (Ireland)

NIGEL HESLOP CELEBRATES SCORING AGAINST THE SCOTS

Hodgkinson had two more shots in that capacious locker to ensure that 15–12, with 20 minutes remaining, finally became 21–12 with goals in the 68th and 74th minutes.

Hodgkinson's haul of 17 points, following 21 against Wales last month, took him to 64 (one try, 29 conversions, 34 penalty goals) in 11 internationals since his debut against Romania in May 1989. No Englishman has been as prolific on the international stage.

England have scored 43 tries in those matches. The aggregate points in the 11 matches, two of which have been lost, are 341 points for, 96 against.

Small wonder the decision not to allow Hodgkinson to kick for goal at all times in last year's Grand Slam/Calcutta Cup/winner-takes-all at Murrayfield will continue to cause blushes in some sectors of the English camp.

This time around Hodgkinson was in expert business well before his first pot at goal. Neither side saw much mileage in running the ball straight, let alone wide. Scotland were snuffed out at the line-out from an early point and precision tactical kicking for position became the order of the day.

While Gavin Hastings, for Scotland, and Hill, for England, mostly found the opposition, Andrew's angles were as acute as they were delicate.

Though, commendably, Scotland were still within reach at 15–12 following a fourth penalty goal by Chalmers, the pressure was always on them to catch up.

Scraps of possession had to be run with the result that some disconcerting cracks that Ian McGeechan, the coach, and his advisers, had papered over, reappeared. Lack of pace is an omission difficult to repair.

Armstrong, Scotland's scrum half, snapped and snarled more competitively – and successfully – than Hill but the back row, for once, was not on song.

Stephen Hilditch, the referee, had an unenviable afternoon and will not, I imagine, greatly enjoy the match video. But he did manage rather better than most of the other 59,299 referees present.

In a match in which the pragmatism put into practice should have delighted the politicians present, as well as the Archbishop of Canterbury, England's

	P	W	D	L	F	A	PTS
ENGLAND	2	2	0	0	46	18	4
FRANCE	2	2	0	0	36	22	4
SCOTLAND	3	1	0	2	53	48	2
IRELAND	2	0	1	1	34	42	1
WALES	3	0	1	2	39	78	1

try was as good as any of the 42 they had scored in their previous ten matches.

The try involved a line-out, two rucks, eight passes and nine players. Ackford started it, Andrew, Richards and Winterbottom gave it impetus and the admirable Heslop, taking Hodgkinson's pass, finished in the south-west corner for his first Championship try.

2 March, Lansdowne Road

UNDERWOOD TRY CROWNS ENGLISH DAY OF TRIUMPH

Ireland 7
England 16

WHEN SOMEONE OF RORY UNDERWOOD'S STANDING says that his try at about 4.07 p.m. against Ireland in Dublin on Saturday was the most important he has scored for England, it is time to take notice. Exaggeration has never been his style.

The modest Underwood, who tops England's all-time list with 26 tries, did not win his country's first Triple Crown for 11 years single-handed – far from it. But in his 42nd international, one short of Tony Neary's English record, he brought the achievement a decided step closer.

The accolades can be spread far and wide among a capable team who, having discovered painfully in the past two years that media co-operation can be a double-edged sword, are fearful of being shown to be overconfident or arrogant.

In overtaking Ireland to win by a goal, a try and two penalty goals to a try and a penalty goal, England were, to borrow the telling phrase of Geoff Cooke, the manager, 'rattled to the teeth'. There was something more than polite interest in the result from Paris, without France's six-try beating of Wales being dwelt upon.

Both managements and players, though, would have been less than human had they not touched briefly on the possible outcome of the Grand Slam match with France at Twickenham on Saturday week.

Ciaran Fitzgerald, the Ireland coach, made no bones about it: 'It is my opinion that France have more options. The English will have to step up on this performance to win at Twickenham and take the Grand Slam.'

Geoff Cooke said: 'It's played three, won three, and all to do with one to go, like last year. As we challenge for the Championship again, we have the advantage of being at Twickenham, not away, as the deciders have been in the last two seasons. We've done well against France in the last couple of years. It's an ideal preparation to face them by being rattled to the teeth.'

Allowing for time added for injuries, England did not lead Ireland until Underwood, executing a delicate scissors with Hodgkinson and accelerating right, then left, struck 10 minutes from the end.

IRELAND 7

J. E. Staples (*London Irish*)

S. Geoghegan (*London Irish*)
B. J. Mullin (*Blackrock*)

D. M. Curtis (*London Irish*)
K. D. Crossan (*Instonians*)

B. A. Smith (*Leicester*)
R. Saunders (*London Irish*) captain

J. J. Fitzgerald (*Young Munster*)
S. J. Smith (*Ballymena*)
D. C. Fitzgerald (*Lansdowne*)

B. J. Rigney (*Greystones*)
N. P. J. Francis (*Blackrock*)

P. M. Matthews (*Wanderers*)
G. F. Hamilton (*NIFC*)
B. F. Robinson (*Ballymena*)

Try: Geoghegan

Penalty goal: B. Smith

ENGLAND 16

S. D. Hodgkinson (*Nottingham*)

N. J. Heslop (*Orrell*)
W. D. C. Carling (*Harlequins*) captain
J. C. Guscott (*Bath*)
R. Underwood (*Leicester & RAF*)

C. R. Andrew (*Wasps*)
R. J. Hill (*Bath*)

J. Leonard (*Harlequins*)
B. C. Moore (*Harlequins*)
J. A. Probyn (*Wasps*)

P. J. Ackford (*Harlequins*)
W. A. Dooley (*Preston Grasshoppers*)

M. C. Teague (*Gloucester*)
P. J. Winterbottom (*Harlequins*)
D. Richards (*Leicester*)

Tries: Underwood, Teague

Conversion: Hodgkinson

Penalty goals: Hodgkinson (2)

Referee: A. Ceccon (France)

Until that point, English nerve ends jangled ceaselessly as Ireland's forwards, gleefully exploiting a freedom which few other international referees would have permitted, piled in, around and over the ball. The lottery launched in the name of the line-out was another fraught area in which English strengths, though not patience, were diluted.

Refereeing eccentricities, though, were only a small part of a highly rewarding match of prolonged passion and fiery fervour. Alain Ceccon, from St Etienne, in his first international, had a limited influence on playing patterns, though while there can be no suggestion of bias, some decisions, mostly against Ireland, were undeniably harsh.

As sometimes happens on such occasions when every sinew is at full stretch, the players sorted out a code of their own; a kind of muscular compromise which, among other things, prevented a vigorous, stressful contest getting out of hand.

Though the wider question of indifferent refereeing standards must be left for the moment, the rugby unions of the 16 participating World Cup nations must be worried. If they are not, they should be. Saturday's evidence was another alarming example in a growing list of unacceptable application and interpretation.

There was a time when a combination of adverse circumstances would have upended England. A variable gusting wind, a slippery, damp surface after eight hours of rain, and some uncharacteristic diffidence after a promising start presented persistent problems. Ireland, with Matthews, Rigney and

RICHARD HILL IN ACTION AGAINST IRELAND IN DUBLIN

Steve Smith to the fore, did not stand on ceremony. Behind them, Saunders, Ireland's scrum half and captain in only his third international, was dexterous and demanding.

Mullin and Curtis, the centres, tackled everything that moved and fullback Staples, one of four London Irish backs in the side, applied basic skills with a dashing boldness and refreshing impudence. Brian Smith, too, had many moments of high skill mixed with wrong options.

For once, the traditional exchange of penalty goals on these occasions was delayed, mostly because Hodgkinson, who began the day with 38 points from two Championship matches this season, missed his first three kicks at goal.

England's goal-kicker put the ball across the face of the posts from the left, hit the near post high above the bar and, in the worst of the wind, floated the ball dead centre but marginally short as it dipped late.

Brian Smith, who kicked the opening penalty goal for Ireland in the 24th minute, was also a fraction short when the ball rebounded off the top of the crossbar.

Hodgkinson levelled with his fourth kick and, immediately after half-time, a drive by Francis and a chip by Mullin set up the position from which, having been held immediately before on the short side, Geoghegan, a rising star, cleverly beat Underwood on half a sixpence.

Despite a second penalty goal by Hodgkinson, English hopes were given a thorough examination for the next 30 minutes. A mixture of inexperience and caution – Saunders stopped kicking and began running, Brian Smith stopped running and resumed kicking – helped England.

The most weighty ballast, though, came from Dooley, Ackford – who was wrongly singled out by a touch-judge for stamping and penalised by the referee – and the back row, of whom Richards, absent throughout last season, was the master. Four English attacks were held deep in Irish territory before another Richards drive and a marvellous low swoop by Andrew set Hodgkinson off on the preliminaries to Underwood's try. Four defenders, including Crossan, who had come across from the opposite wing, and Geoghegan, were left floundering.

Leonard, Hill, Andrew and Teague attended to the second try in the final seconds, and Hodgkinson's conversion deep from the right-hand touch took him to 46 points this season, two more than Dusty Hare's English record.

	P	W	D	L	F	A	PTS
FRANCE	3	3	0	0	72	25	6
ENGLAND	3	3	0	0	62	25	6
SCOTLAND	3	1	0	2	53	48	2
IRELAND	3	0	1	2	41	58	1
WALES	4	0	1	3	42	114	1

16 March, Twickenham

ENGLAND FULFIL THEIR DREAMS AS FRENCH FALL AT LAST THROW

England 21
France 19

FOR THE MOMENT ENGLAND'S PLAYERS, management and back-up team deserve to enjoy the vanity of victory. A first Grand Slam for 11 years demands celebration – and the recognition of the sustained capabilities of the best side in the 1991 Championship.

In treasuring so rare an achievement for English rugby in recent years, the occasion was given a further dimension of scalp-tingling excitement – or was it apprehension? – by the inventive daring of France, who won universal admiration but not the match.

If the analogy of the sturdy shire horse in competition with the thoroughbred racehorse is less than kind to England, possibly the more acceptable version would be the no-nonsense, feet-on-the ground battering ram versus the subtle, spring-heeled swordsman.

What cannot conceivably be in dispute is that the Save & Prosper Grand Slam decider between England and France at Twickenham on Saturday will be fondly remembered as an epic struggle expertly refereed and crammed full of drama, high skill and pulsating entertainment.

If that were not sufficient on an afternoon of slate grey skies and a worsening dripping drizzle, the French presented a rapt full house with two tries of superlative quality. Fact made a monkey of fiction yet again.

Satisfying as the counter thrust which culminated in Rory Underwood's 27th international try was, for once England's record-breaking wing three-quarter has to be among the also-rans. Nor has that anything to do with magnanimity or humility in victory.

France twice tore up the international rugby safety instructions which declare that Thou Shalt Not run the ball out from deep defence – and never from behind your own line. As Twickenham twice caught its collective breath, the runners soared into areas momentarily unguarded. They had won time and found space.

That combination, as England knew full well beforehand, would be their undoing if allowed to persist. Twice in 80 minutes they could not shut down

ENGLAND 21

S. D. Hodgkinson (*Nottingham*)

N. J. Heslop (*Orrell*)
W. D. C. Carling (*Harlequins*) captain
J. C. Guscott (*Bath*)
R. Underwood (*Leicester & RAF*)

C. R. Andrew (*Wasps*)
R. J. Hill (*Bath*)

J. Leonard (*Harlequins*)
B. C. Moore (*Harlequins*)
J. A. Probyn (*Wasps*)

P. J. Ackford (*Harlequins*)
W. A. Dooley (*Preston Grasshoppers*)

M. C. Teague (*Gloucester*)
P. J. Winterbottom (*Harlequins*)
D. Richards (*Leicester*)

Try: Underwood

Conversion: Hodgkinson

Dropped goal: Andrew

Penalty goals: Hodgkinson (4)

FRANCE 19

S. Blanco (*Biarritz*)

J.-B. Lafond (*Racing*)
P. Sella (*Agen*)
F. Mesnel (*Racing*)
P. Saint-André (*Montferrand*)

D. Camberabero (*Beziers*)
P. Berbizier (*Agen*)

G. Lascubé (*Agen*)
P. Marocco (*Montferrand*)
P. Ondarts (*Biarritz*)

M. Tachdjian (*Racing*)
O. Roumat (*Dax*)

X. Blond (*Racing*)
L. Cabannes (*Racing*)
A. Benazzi (*Agen*)

Replacements: M. Cecillon (*Bourgoin*) for Tachdjian (55 mins)

Tries: Saint-André, Camberabero, Mesnel

Conversions: Camberabero (2)

Penalty goal: Camberabero

Referee: L. J. Peard (Wales)

RORY UNDERWOOD SCORES
ENGLAND'S TRY AGAINST THE FRENCH

EST
TTER
COURAGE

that threat, the effects of which were two tries of startling ingenuity and invention by Saint-André and Mesnel – and a match that will be enshrined in the folk-lore of the game.

Blanco, Lafond, Sella and Camberabero in the 12th minute, and Berbizier, Sella and Blanco in the 79th, created tries of which dreams are made. The first covered 100 metres or more, beginning when Blanco ran the ball back from a failed penalty goal kick by Hodgkinson.

The second, with England sitting comfortably on a 21–13 lead deep in French territory, Grand Slam sweaters and ties at the ready, started in-field on the north-west side of the pitch, Berbizier circling into open spaces.

Two more passes left Mesnel with his sights on the south-east corner and what was left of the cover to beat. Hill, having sensed the danger, covered across as Mesnel came at him.

There appeared no way past, yet the efficient Hill was left stranded, so mesmerised by the jink, shuffle, body lean and change of pace. Camberabero converted from the touchline and at 21–19, the Cup was all but dashed from eager English lips.

Earlier, borrowing a leaf from England's book, the French reminded themselves that there were more customary ways of scoring tries, not that the Grand Slam champions have any cause to apologise for their scoring methods.

Such recriminations as there were must be reserved for Blond, the French flanker, whose hot-headed foolishness ruined what chances the team may have had of victory.

For the second of their three tries France cobbled together the only forward drive of consequence they managed throughout. Twice the maul rolled forward, the second time with conviction.

Cecillon, the replacement lock for Tachdjian, was in the van and when halted the ball was rapidly re-presented. Camberabero chipped high to the south-west corner, got there first and, amid a gaggle of bodies, snaffled the ball to score himself.

Yet for all the expertise of the tries, England's victory by a goal, dropped goal and four penalty goals to two goals, try and penalty goal was their third in succession over France.

The England forwards made everything possible, though they, too, have

	P	W	D	L	F	A	PTS
ENGLAND	4	4	0	0	83	44	8
FRANCE	4	3	0	1	91	46	6
SCOTLAND	4	2	0	2	81	73	4
IRELAND	4	0	1	3	66	86	1
WALES	4	0	1	3	42	114	1

good cause to be immensely grateful to Hodgkinson, who weighed in with another 14 points, and to Underwood, whose 43rd cap matched Tony Neary's all-time England record.

In 13 internationals Hodgkinson, who made his England debut in May 1989 against Romania in Bucharest, has scored 186 points – 40 penalty goals, 31 conversions and a try. His 60 championship points this season, which include a world-record seven penalty goals against Wales in January, erase the previous Five Nations' record of 54 points by Jean-Patrick Lescarboura.

Not everything went for Hodgkinson on Saturday. He missed five of nine penalty kicks at goal and when under fire in the first half, deliberately tossed the ball into touch – an offence which enabled Camberabero to put over the penalty kick from an awkward angle to level the score at 9–9.

For all that, there was ample consolation, quite apart from those 60 championship points. It was Hodgkinson, the player who is said to be slow about the field, who provided Underwood with the try-scoring pass after 30 minutes.

Teague and Richards smartly dealt with the preliminaries, and with Carling making the diagonal thrust from outside half, Andrew was next in line. Hodgkinson was there on cue and Underwood, having eased almost to a jog before stepping on the accelerator, ran away from Lafond.

England's other points came from a dropped goal in the 17th minute by Andrew which owed much to the masterly control of the forwards. If such a thing were possible in so demanding an encounter, physically and mentally, Ackford and company provided their half backs with an armchair ride.

When it comes to the nuts and bolts of basic requirements, of discipline, of control, France, who were restricted to six scrum put-ins, acquired a painful though pertinent demonstration of what must be done to secure a World Cup.

Blanco, the captain, said as much many times over afterwards – and in his farewell appearance in a Championship match was unstinting in his praise of England, whom he described as honourable champions and gentlemen. Quite right, too.

TWICKENHAM MATCH FACTS

SCORING SEQUENCE

2m	Hodgkinson penalty *Ruck offence*	E	3–0
12m	Saint-André try *Blanco running from behind his own line*	F	4–3
13m	Camberabero conversion *From in front of goal*	F	6–3
17m	Andrew drop goal *From ruck ball in front of posts*	E	6–6
23m	Hodgkinson penalty *Ruck offence*	E	9–6
27m	Camberabero penalty *Deliberate throw into touch*	F	9–9
30m	Underwood try *Swerved outside opponent for corner try*	E	13–9
31m	Hodgkinson conversion *Kicked ten metres from touchline*	E	15–9
34m	Hodgkinson penalty *Foul play at maul*	E	18–9
56m	Camberabero try *Dived on loose ball from chip ahead*	F	13–18
63m	Hodgkinson penalty *Argument with referee after a maul*	E	21–13
78m	Mesnel try *25-metre run along touchline after an attack from his own 22*	F	17–21
79m	Camberabero conversion *Kicked from touchline*	F	19–21

BREAKDOWN OF PLAY

(England scores first)

1	Tries	3
1	Conversions	2
4	Penalties	1
1	Dropped goals	0
16	Scrums with head	5
0	Scrums against head	0
12	Line-outs with throw	10
7	Line-outs against throw	5
16	Decisive rucks	9
13	Decisive mauls	7

- England's Grand Slam was their first since 1980 and their ninth since 1910.
- England fielded an unchanged side throughout the Five Nations' Championship for only the second time. The previous occasion was in 1960 when England shared the Championship with France.
- Rory Underwood played his 43rd major Test to join Tony Neary as England's most capped player.
- For the first time since 1965 England have won three consecutive matches against France.
- Simon Hodgkinson set new records for most penalties (18) and most points (60) in a championship season. Top scorers in a season are:

Pts	Player	Season
60	S. Hodgkinson (E)	1991
54	J.-P. Lescarboura (F)	1984
52	O. Campbell (I)	1983
52	P. Thorburn (W)	1986
52	G. Hastings (S)	1986
50	P. Dods (S)	1984
47	M. Kiernan (I)	1985
46	O. Campbell (I)	1980
46	O. Campbell (I)	1982
46	C. Chalmers (S)	1991
46	D. Camberabero (F)	1991

Chapter Four

ENGLAND'S POST-MATCH PRESS CONFERENCE

By CHRIS JONES

WILL CARLING: 'IT IS ALMOST impossible to put it into words. We haven't had time to think. It's lovely to be part of such a successful set-up. It is many things at once. It will take a far more eloquent person than me to put it into words.'

Simon Hodgkinson: 'All the games this season have been one-offs as the Championship has progressed. Wales was very emotional. The necessity to beat Scotland after last year. The narrow escape against Ireland. And today the Grand Slam. I feel I speak for all the players when I say it is more relief having got the burden of all that out of the way.'

Geoff Cooke: 'The French did what we always thought they were capable of – magical running from all over the field. If you turn your back for an instant you are likely to be punished. We were punished but got away with it. Irritation that we had dropped our guard when it should have been three points to us and instead it was six to the French with that first try. The players probably felt the same because they had dropped their guard. I would prefer to have scored it rather than have them score against us.'

Will Carling: 'It takes time to come to terms with everything. There are some very tired people in the dressing-room. A lot of pressure, anxiety – it takes time. You cannot just snap out of it. There will be a big party tonight.'

Roger Uttley: 'The last Grand Slam was a big game and this was a big game. I was delighted our players were able to come out on top against a very good French side. It is immensely satisfying for all concerned. There is a sense of great relief that four matches have been won.'

Geoff Cooke: 'It was a great achievement for England. The players worked very hard and it's now in the record books. We have now completed phase one of the year. Everybody will enjoy it the next time we get together and then we will look at the result.'

NIGEL HESLOP AND RORY UNDERWOOD REFLECT ON ENGLAND'S GRAND SLAM

Will Carling: 'I think we have a tremendous ball-winning capacity, strong defence and we have very powerful runners. We are a very well-balanced side at the moment and very hungry to win. The French showed they were lethal on the break and we missed opportunities. In days to come we will be disappointed about that, but we did enough and we won and that's what we will remember.'

Roger Uttley: 'France fought England every inch of the way and one of the great strengths of this England team is that they have the capacity to play the game for the full duration with an intensity that I find amazing. The players deserve all the plaudits they have worked so hard for.'

Geoff Cooke: 'We would not have missed this for the world and I think I speak for everyone when I say that. You have to understand that the emotion of being involved in something like this is quite amazing and you feel an overwhelming sense of relief. We have gone out and done what we planned and for the people who watched that it was a thrilling experience.'

Will Carling: 'When you are expected to win, and England were expected to win the Grand Slam, it's a sense of relief because we felt we would win. If we had gone through the Championship as underdogs we would be jumping around. We have won it and feel relieved. I enjoy winning. Internationals are incredible pressure.'

Geoff Cooke: 'We have got the platform we wanted because we have won something and that puts us in a good frame of mind. We will go into the World Cup as European and Five Nations' champions and that is important. But it is a new competition and our aim is to qualify by going through the pool rounds in the best possible way. That is a long way off yet. Obviously we are working towards the future, but we lost two B games. But you're not looking to transpose a whole side forward, just four or five players. I'm reasonably optimistic we are moving on the right track.'

Simon Hodgkinson: 'Obviously I was disappointed to miss two relatively easy ones in front of the posts and that is what people will probably remember and write about. But, having gone through the Championship and beaten Lescarboura's record and the team actually winning, which was the prime objective today, I'm absolutely delighted. It is something we will reflect on in days to come. We have won the Triple Crown and Grand Slam and so we now are a team that are capable of winning things. We will not be labelled the team that almost made it.'

Daniel Dubroca: 'England won because of the 80 minutes of pressure they put on. When you lack quality possession, all you can do is try to score the tries we did.'

Chapter Five

SEEN AND HEARD

By BARRIE FAIRALL

BREATHLESS FROM THE BATTLE, England's triumphant players were soon asked for their verdict on the encounter with the French. First in front of the BBC cameras came Brian Moore. 'It was a hard game. I don't know what it was like to watch, but it was fast and it was furious and it was physical. I'm very glad we held on to the end because last year we wouldn't have done that. This year there was a better atmosphere. There was more steel and I think we deserved it in the end.'

Captain Will Carling followed his hooker to the microphone. 'They were lethal, you know, as they showed. But I thought our forwards, as they played all season, were absolutely superb. The discipline they have now and the control, it's incredible. I think they've proved themselves, if not the best pack, then certainly one that's going to cause a lot of problems in the World Cup.'

The try-scoring Rory Underwood said: 'Teams have tried to stop us playing. We've played away at Cardiff trying to beat the hoodoo, played against a Scottish side that tried to stop you running the ball and against an Irish side away from home, which is never easy. We were home today against a French side obviously determined, but luckily for us we just managed to hold them off.'

Simon Hodgkinson, who had kicked his way into the record books, then added: 'I suppose the only problem that we had was that sometimes we had too many people there and people were getting in each other's way and the ball was spilling in the rainy conditions. Today, a win's a win and we are just absolutely delighted. There's been a hell of a lot of pressure on us from the media, a lot of expectancy from family, friends and fans. It was the worst 80 minutes of my life and I'm just pleased it's over.'

In the studio, meanwhile, for *Rugby Special*, Jamie Salmon was summing up the situation: 'The England crowd had been waiting 11 years for a finale such as this and 60,000 people had gone home very, very happy. Before the game the atmosphere was alive, during it and then again at the end when it all came right for England. It was a marvellous day out, a great victory for the players. They had worked incredibly hard over a number of years without the reward. Now they've finally got it and they should be enjoying themselves.'

Asked how it was for a Scotsman, Ian Robertson admitted: 'I was delighted that England at last have got their due reward because they had two near misses the last two seasons. This time they were also under pressure again and even at the end it looked as if France might steal it. But there is a much stronger backbone to this England side. Their organisation and discipline is tremendous and they did everything right. It was a great occasion for them. At the end, to see them chaired off, half the team put on the shoulders of the crowd, it showed the relief.'

'I think more than the development of a great England side,' commented Eddie Butler, 'the miracle is that Twickenham has taken over from Cardiff as the centre of rugby in the British Isles. As long as they keep it going, with the packaging so good and making it so attractive, then really British rugby will flourish. It's just a shame that it is at the expense of the Welsh. It has all changed and it's a great day out, a great circus, and sport in general needs that sort of atmosphere.'

Asked by Chris Rea about specifics and where England won the match, Salmon said: 'It started up front and finished up front. The back row has had a marvellous Championship and Richards has been a colossus in everything he has done, which has enabled Hill and Andrew to control the pace of the game and force errors from the French. The backs didn't have a lot to do but the one real chance they got Underwood finished it off superbly. Hodgkinson had a mixed day in terms of his goal-kicking, but he's learnt and gone a step further in his performances this year. I think the whole squad has gelled together so well. It's a tribute to them and the work they have done to finish it off.'

In his tactical appreciation of the game, Robertson opined that: 'We expected England to have the edge in the scrum, but they were more solid and won better quality scrum ball. At the line-out, they again won more ball of better quality. But the key thing was the loose, the open, the mauls. They were always driving forward. They were in low body positions, pumping away and they were gaining five yards in every one of the rucks and mauls. Always they were driving France backwards and France on the retreat we know are nothing like as good as France on the attack. And Hill and Andrew put up a load of high kicks, turning the French and driving up towards Blanco, who was just surrounded by a white wall of English jerseys. That kept the momentum and the rhythm going the whole time.'

Butler, a dedicated follower of France all season and commenting on what Rea suggested was not one of the better French performances, said: 'That was simply because the English forwards were so good. Along with the New Zealanders, England have developed this new system in rugby of using the

JAMIE SALMON: 'NOW THEY'VE FINALLY GOT IT, THEY SHOULD BE ENJOYING THEMSELVES'

rolling maul as the one place to drain the opposition. The set scrum is no longer that important. All the damage is coming from this rolling maul with Richards and Teague and really nobody does it better.'

Rea pointed out that the French had nevertheless provided the dishes of the day. 'Given that they were so comprehensively beaten up front,' Butler said, 'they were still capable of running from absolutely everywhere. Serge Blanco had a nightmare in the middle of two moments of sheer brilliance. The audacity to run from behind his posts so early in the game, going through the sticky patches of dropping the ball, having his kicks charged down, and just to come up in the last minute and make that try-scoring break.'

Robertson agreed that England always had the strength to come back. 'I think it was a tactical triumph for Roger Uttley, Will Carling and the whole team. And don't forget Rory Underwood's try. He didn't get many chances, but he took it brilliantly and that lifted the whole England team.'

Also coming in for some praise was the referee, Les Peard. 'Very sympathetic understanding of the whole atmosphere,' was how Robertson summed up the Welshman's part in the proceedings. 'He did have to wag the finger two or three times at errant Frenchmen, but he kept the whole spirit of the game going and the movement and the flow of it. I thought he had an excellent game.'

And the last word on the Championship season fell to Butler. 'Well, there was an outstanding Welshman on the international field, and that was Les Peard!'

Chapter Six

PICK OF THE PEN

By BARRIE FAIRALL

ON OCCASIONS SUCH AS THIS, those once fondly referred to as 'Fleet Street's finest' swing into action. And, in England's finest hour, what better way to sum up their achievements than to turn to the pages of the national newspapers for a sample of what the game's leading writers had in store for us at the conclusion of this Grand Slam season.

Writing in *The Sunday Times*, Stephen Jones said:

> It was fabulous. It was Twickenham's loudest and most tumultuous day and a game to rank with any in the history of the Five Nations' tournament.
>
> France scored three tries to one, the first of them the most wonderful score the old-new stadium has ever seen, and England won the most deeply coveted and, in a way, the most concrete of mythical trophies ever awarded in sport – the Grand Slam and the championship title itself to add to the Triple Crown.
>
> They did it with leonine hearts and the most ferocious commitment and application. They also did it with real skills and wit. They were marshalled expertly by Hill and Andrew at half-back, and some of the kicking of this pair was inch-perfect as the ball rained down on Blanco and the French wings. Both England flankers contributed herculean efforts, and there was yet another dazzling demonstration of the finishing arts of Underwood.
>
> Yet if England did not have to sweat quite as profusely as the final score might suggest, they were given a titanic battle by a team at least 18 months away from any sort of peak. There was hardly anything in the French performance of which they could not be proud, bar isolated outbursts of temper and handling errors brought about by their sheer ambition and energy.
>
> They scored two brilliant tries, their attitude was on the heroic side of wholesome, and Blanco, that stupendous man, wonderful attacker and ambassador, marked what everyone felt would be his final appearance at Twickenham with a Blanco-like performance. On the other hand, if France continue to improve, they could easily be back at Twickenham, Blanco and all, in the November World Cup final.

> In the last analysis they did not quite have the forward platform, and they did not quite have the technical discipline needed so sorely when up against a kicker like Hodgkinson and a team so determined to cash in on errors.
>
> Blond in the back row was a chief culprit, but there was a mighty effort in the lineout from Roumat and Benazzi, and the tall Moroccan had a game of world class all over the field.
>
> There is equally good news about the one neutral on the field, because Mr Peard contributed exactly the right measure of control and sympathy the world of international rugby has been seeking from its referees for some time. There was a consistency about him, and he even appeared to be having a little fun.

In *The Independent on Sunday*, the former Scottish international Chris Rea wrote:

> It is rare enough in the annals of rugby football to have everything hinging on the final match of the international season. But to have a spectacle and a climax such as the one at Twickenham yesterday is indeed a sporting privilege. It will almost certainly not go down as one of the great tactical masterpieces but for raw excitement it could not be improved upon. The French tries alone will live long in the memory but when the final whistle blew with just two points separating the sides, both of them on the edge of exhaustion, it was England's day just as it has been England's season.
>
> Their single-minded pursuit of the ultimate prize in European rugby has been crowned with success and, despite France's spectacular final flourish which brought them so close, England's victory was thoroughly deserved. The pattern of the play was entirely in line with most of the pre-match predictions. England's forward effort was of such controlled savagery that there were times when it seemed that the French were on the point of disintegration. Only the remarkable Benazzi stood defiantly in the way of England's incessant charges led by Richards, Teague and Winterbottom. In the lineout too Benazzi did as much as any Frenchman to disrupt the mastery of Ackford and Dooley.
>
> Hodgkinson managed to overhaul Lescarboura's record number of points in an international season and Underwood, once again with meagre rations, produced enough fuel to slip his marker for his 27th try for England. No matter that the *plat du jour* was served up by the French. England, with overwhelming territorial advantage were, apart from the final minutes of almost stupefying intensity, in control.

Accompanying Rea at Twickenham was the columnist Brough Scott, who began:

> At the end they carried Will Carling above the shouting, above the crowd. He and his team can go into legend. They deserved their Grand Slam, but here they will always be remembered for beating the sublime.
>
> For as long as people talk about this match – and it will live down the

SIMON HODGKINSON OVERHAULED LESCARBOURA'S RECORD NUMBER OF POINTS IN AN INTERNATIONAL SEASON

centuries – they will first talk about that extraordinary, stunning, unbelievable, breathtaking try by France. We had been promised moments of Blanco magic, but this, his opening touch, for the ball to go the whole length of the stadium before Saint-André scored. It wasn't just *incroyable*. There wasn't a soul in the stadium who didn't bless themselves to be alive.

England won it. England were magnificent, relentless, brave, fast and true. But France made it. Made it by their brilliance. By that extraordinary potential that took us right down to the wire.

As the sodden crowd drifted merrily away one tricolour-draped French fan produced a trumpet from inside his coat, turned towards us and blew a flawless version of *Auld Lang Syne*. It was that sort of day.

Another former international, *The Observer*'s Clem Thomas, noted:

It may have been spring in Paris but it was winter for France as England exorcised the spectre of failure which has hung over their accomplished team for the last three years. They can now at last bask in the glory of winning a Grand Slam which has taken them into a 9–8 lead of Slams over Wales, and which perhaps will unleash them from their defensive attitudes.

England could not complain on this occasion that their opponents were negative, for France managed to show a Gallic deftness, an elegance of running, a grace and a skill which are perhaps beyond the reach of Anglo-Saxons. France not only scored three tries to one; their first try was probably the greatest scored in the Five Nations' Championship, a masterpiece of derring-do and versatility.

If the French possessed the greater artistry, they did not have the England pack, who again did the business by denying their opponents the possession, with which one dreads to think what they might have achieved. The England forwards were, as expected, the means by which England choked France to death. They denied them and banged them about so much that occasionally they lost composure.

It was perhaps the French propensity for over-eagerness and over-excitement in the rucks and mauls which were their principal undoing. Xavier Blond, the flanker, grabbed the Welsh referee, Les Peard, by the jersey in a threatening gesture. He was lucky to stay on the pitch.

It is always difficult to give individual praise to England's supreme pack, for throughout this season and again here they produced a collective performance which was beyond reproach. No pack, in my memory, has earned the Grand Slam more. They must surely go down as one of the great packs, if not the greatest, in England's history.

Backing up Thomas was Geoffrey Nicholson, who said:

The criticism of England for playing too narrow a game, for relying on Simon Hodgkinson's place-kicking, for running things too close in every sense – that is all academic now. The Grand Slam is theirs again after 11 years and champions don't have to make excuses for themselves.

MIKE TEAGUE LEADS THE TACKLE ON SERGE BLANCO

It is the French who need to make the explanations. In particular, why did they allow the opportunities to slip away through lack of discipline?

Leslie Peard is not the most draconian of referees: he was especially lenient with Xavier Blond, who might well have been sent off for grabbing his jersey when he was already pacing out an extra ten metres for dissent to a penalty. But neither is Peard a soft touch, and the French brought many of their troubles on themselves.

John Taylor, who, like Thomas, once played for Wales, stated in the *Mail on Sunday* :

At last England have fulfilled their promise and their dream.

At the third attempt they have swept the board as the Grand Slam and the Championship were yesterday added to the Triple Crown and the Calcutta Cup.

All the frustrations of the last 11 years, and the previous two seasons in particular, were swept aside as England set themselves up as the main challengers to New Zealand in next autumn's World Cup.

In a sublime match – French flair pitted against English grit and determination from start to finish – England kept their resolve, played their best rugby of the season and emerged triumphant. But it was as close as the score suggests.

Once again England forwards were giants, even among international rugby players. They had to fight harder than ever before to take control up front but eventually they achieved it.

Dean Richards and Mike Teague mixed things up beautifully, sometimes driving the ball back in to set up a rolling maul, but sometimes releasing it quickly so that, for the first time this season, the backs had some space in which to run.

Half the forwards knew this was their last chance of a Grand Slam and nothing was going to deny them, even when nerves got to Simon Hodgkinson and he missed five out of ten kicks at goal, two from simple positions.

Writing in the same paper, Patrick Collins said:

There were no ribbons, no bows and only a few frills. But even when it arrives in a plain brown wrapper, a Grand Slam is welcome and wonderful.

As the English supporters capered beneath grey and glowering Twickenham skies, they cared little about the manner, nor the hairsbreadth margin of victory.

The long seasons of frustration had been buried. The ploughboys had defeated the poets. And Will Carling's men had come into their kingdom.

If the game of Rugby Union should still feel the need to promote its virtues, then it could do no better than replay this awesomely compelling match at every opportunity. In particular, it should replay a first-half bulging

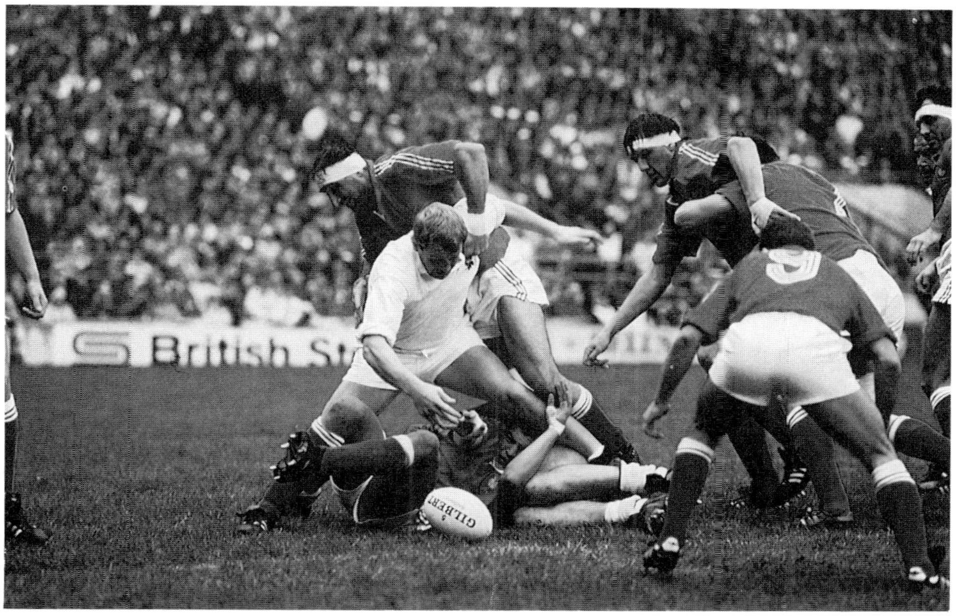

DEAN RICHARDS WEIGHS IN AGAINST TACHDJIAN AND BENAZZI OF FRANCE

with enterprise, flair, and the kind of heart-stopping excitement which left the whole of Twickenham, fans along with players, hopelessly exhausted.

England had obeyed their pragmatic instincts; rucking, mauling and driving forward with a pack as formidable as any who have ever reached out for a Grand Slam.

The pre-match hyperbole had invoked Agincourt and Waterloo, and men like Richards, Dooley, Ackford and Teague seemed to have taken such rhetoric at face value as they hurled themselves into combat. For once, though, the backs were not entirely forgotten. We were made aware of the potency which lurked outside after half-an-hour when the ball was quickly released and whipped along the line for Rory Underwood to evade his marker for a soothing try.

Yet if that score was admirable, it had to suffer by comparison with a try the French had conjured 18 minutes earlier. Serge Blanco, in his last championship match, instigated the affair from beneath his posts. The dazzling runners were deployed one after another; Sella, Lafond and, most entrancingly, Camberabero. A chip and catch, a cross-kick which simply reeked with class, and there was Saint-André, surging beneath the posts for a try which even the boomingly partisan Twickenham audience could only stand and cheer.

Come the Monday and Steve Bale wrote in *The Independent*:

Grand achievements take a while to sink in and if there is surprise from some who know no better that the English mood after the grandest day of their rugby lives is exhaustion rather than ecstasy, they should refer to past winners. They will tell you it takes hindsight to appreciate how precious Grand Slams are.

The numbness of sheer relief is well remembered by Phil Bennett from 1978 and Jim Aitken from 1984 – captains whose Welsh and Scottish teams beat the French on previous winner-takes-all occasions. Now it is Will Carling's moment to savour the chance to lie back at last and while he relaxes think of anything but England.

He will not have long. In this World Cup year, the demand on players is more persistent than it has ever been, and if England were to lose on tour in Fiji and Australia in four months, their first Grand Slam, Triple Crown and Five Nations' title since 1980, and only the third since the war, would become instant history.

This is not being churlish, merely as realistic as the England players need to be as the rest of the most momentous year they will ever experience stretches ahead. Consider the fate of the Welsh team who wore the Triple Crown in 1988 – from champions to also-rans in the space of two thumpings by the All Blacks – and you realise the transience of success.

Which is not to say the culmination of almost four years' work since England's ignominious retreat from the last World Cup is not worth the loudest celebration. Over the past two months, we have witnessed a heroic effort by one of the most durable and efficient packs assembled in international rugby to squeeze most of the life out of all their opponents.

If this has not led to total asphyxiation – and the opportunity to turn forward pressure into a three-quarter runabout like the Welsh often managed in the 1970s – it has been mainly because of the stubbornness of the opposition, even of the now-embattled Welsh. England correctly saw that the main chance lay in their forwards and seized it.

Meanwhile, Alan Fraser, *The Independent*'s columnist, mentioned:

Even before the victorious English players had left the hallowed turf – and it took Simon Hodgkinson fully 15 minutes to swim across a sea of unprecedented emotion – the electronic scoreboard at Twickenham revealed a flashing sign of the times. 'Official . . . Grand Slam Ties . . . Jumpers. Orders,' the three-lined whip cracked at customers only too eager to buy mementoes of a great occasion.

There followed, with almost indecent delay, a simple message: 'Congratulations England'. Exhausted players, mentally and physically drained from their efforts during the Championship campaign, would have been too excited and too relieved to notice the priority. Marketing, too, had won the day.

In *The Times*, David Hands said:

Twickenham was twice blessed on Saturday: nearly 59,000 spectators saw England win the Grand Slam and Five Nations' Championship for which their players have so heart-achingly yearned this season and they also

PETER WINTERBOTTOM AND RICHARD HILL DISPLAY SYNCHRONISED RUNNING AGAINST THE FRENCH

witnessed the lethal French running that embellished a marvellous sporting occasion with two of the great tries.

Perhaps, when the euphoria and emotion of the occasion – England's first championship success for 11 years – has dwindled into the background, the players will remember, above all, that they took part in just that – a sporting occasion. There was no meanness to spoil the day, but a fast, furious competition which England deserved to win by a goal, four penalty goals and a dropped goal to two goals, a try and a penalty. But not before France had shaken them to their boots.

Albert Ferrasse, the French president, jested at the post-match banquet that his country will press at the International Board meeting this week for the try to be worth six points, and to make it retrospective – the point about the penalty against the try was never better illustrated than when Sella was caught scrabbling on the wrong side of a ruck under his own posts. But for that, England might have scored the try which Andrew's beautiful steepling kick and Guscott's catch so nearly created.

If you break the laws, you pay the penalty and, in Les Peard, the match had a referee fit for the occasion. The Welsh police traffic instructor laid out his guidelines from the first minute and the players responded. If Hodgkinson had kicked at goal with the metronomic accuracy which was his in the first half of the championship – he missed five penalty attempts, two from in front of the posts – England could have been out of sight.

Robert Armstrong, in *The Guardian*, took the line:

England moved beyond the pale of criticism – for the moment – and into the annals of history by winning the Grand Slam with a ruthlessly methodical victory over France at rainswept Twickenham. At a stroke Will Carling's men not only banished the bitter disappointment of previous championships but blasted out a warning that they are ready to take on all comers in the World Cup next autumn.

No England side surely have pursued the Holy Grail of a Slam with such ambition, and almost certainly no English pack has swept aside the opposition with such a potent sense of collective rigour. Despite scoring three tries to one the French rightly insisted that England were worthy champions if only because their forwards exerted awesome pressure throughout 83 minutes.

If England supplied the consistent power that wins matches, France displayed the breathtaking audacity, the sheer brio that prompts spectators to leap out of their seats in acclamation. While this absorbing contest was not quite a classic, France's skilful backs reminded us time and again that no coaching strategy can legislate for moments of outrageous genius.

The immediate question raised by England's hard-won success is whether they have the resources to establish a lengthy period of ascendancy such as France have achieved in Europe, and New Zealand across the world. Carling's side may indeed go far in the World Cup, but it remains to be seen to what extent the structure and depth of the English game will stand up to the international demands of the 1990s. The going can only get harder.

And, for a description of THAT try, how about Frank Keating's *Guardian* offering?

> Four momentous tries gilded Saturday's climax, with the first possibly the most opulent since old men with memories were themselves at their grandfather's knee. That takes in all the rich history of the Five Nations' Championship.
>
> The very context sharpened the grandeur of its daring, dotty conception and the nerveless joy of its execution. For the challenge, in bold relief, matched England's substance, nous and penalty power against France's airy elan, spontaneity and dextrous tricks and treats.
>
> At once the two philosophies collided. England missed a long penalty and all eyes and senses, certainly those of the England XV for a moment, relaxed and prepared for a 22 drop-out.
>
> Suddenly all hell broke loose or, rather, the incomparable Blanco, dusky warrior-captain of France, did. 'Moi, moi,' he shouted to Saint-André. Blanco has always put his trust in gods who favour the foolhardy. He was now across his line but still only ten yards into England's territory. In a trice the ball was with Mesnel outside him and the centre's left hip took out Andrew, first to spot the danger, and an instantaneous finger-tip pass allowed Sella, at speed, to round his own despairing white marker.
>
> Sella was over the 22 and momentarily clear as England regrouped and frantically funnelled back. The stalwart Probyn had tanked across to confront him on the ten-metre line. Sella feinted to knife inside him, so stopping the prop in his tracks, and, as he did so, he turned in a dummy-scissors loop and fed on the outside again the delicate Camberabero. The pit-a-pat fly-half could now snipe across the halfway mark.
>
> Then, with dainty exactness, he slippered the ball over the head of the retreating Hodgkinson, caught it in full-pelt stride and was now up to England's 22-metre flag. Though England's bold general Carling had remarkably made it across the field he could only fling himself at Camberabero a split-second after the Frenchman had dapped the most perfect cross-kick to within five metres of the posts.
>
> This took out the corner-flagging Hill and left Saint-André to compose himself, collect and triumphantly launch himself at the line as Guscott's all-in, last-gasp dive lassoed his ankles. The palpitating thing was done.
>
> From line to line it took 17.25 seconds, four more than the previous collective marvel of the age, for the Barbarians at Cardiff on 27 January 1973, when the dancing Bennett dared and set in train that breathtaking passage down another touchline. For Dawes's phoney dummy then, read Sella's phoney scissors here; for Quinnell's genius slip-catch from David then, here was Camberabero's chip-and-catch.
>
> But that Barbarians epic was done with licence to cavort. If daring failed, no matter. Saturday's audacious try was inspired by all the vivid intensity of the grandeur of the Slam.

AND THE HEADLINES

SATURDAY, 16 MARCH

FIRST 15 MINUTES CRUCIAL FOR ENGLAND
EARLY SKIRMISHES WILL DETERMINE HOW BADLY FRANCE WANT GRAND SLAM
UNDERWOOD TIMES RECORD APPEARANCE TO PERFECTION
STAR OF BLANCO HANGS OVER THE TWICKENHAM 'TEMPLE'

The Daily Telegraph

ENGLAND TOO DEDICATED TO BE DENIED
HODGKINSON AIMS HIGH
COACHES PLUMP FOR ENGLAND
EVEN FOR THE FRENCH, THE RESULT IS NOW EVERYTHING
A POWERHOUSE OF SILENT STRENGTH (DEAN RICHARDS)

The Times

FRENCH HAPPY TO RELAX
ENGLAND TAKE THEIR FINAL CLAIM TO HEADQUARTERS
CARLING TAKES THE STRAIN ON A PATH TO GLORY

The Independent

JEFF PROBYN AND JASON LEONARD
COME TO GRIPS WITH FRANCK MESNEL

SUNDAY, 17 MARCH

ENGLAND SURGE TO THE SLAM
POWER, PASSION AND SOMETHING INCROYABLE

The Independent on Sunday

ENGLAND'S SWEETEST TRIUMPH
FRENCH HAVE NO EXCUSE

The Observer

ENGLAND BLAST FRENCH BLUNDERS
FORWARDS AGAIN THE DRIVING FORCE FOR GRAND SLAM

Sunday Telegraph

ENGLISH HEART TRIUMPHS OVER GALLIC FLAIR FOR GRAND SLAM

The Sunday Times

ENGLAND SLAM THE BRAKES ON FRANCE
IT'S CARLING'S KINGDOM

Mail on Sunday

MONDAY, 18 MARCH

ENGLAND DO IT IN THE GRAND STYLE
PLAYERS CARRIED HOME BY FANS' SWEET CHARIOT
GLORYING IN THOSE CLOSE ENCOUNTERS OF TWO TOTALLY DIFFERENT KINDS
ENGLAND FULFIL THEIR DREAMS AS FRENCH FALL AT LAST THROW
A PROUD DAY TO SAY: 'I WAS THERE'

The Daily Telegraph

ENGLAND'S HEROIC FORWARD MARCH
CHAMPIONS RACING TO ENTER THE VIDEO AGE
WORLD CUP IS LURE FOR ENGLISH

The Independent

MAGNIFICENT ENGLAND RISE TO THE OCCASION
GLORY BELONGS TO FRANCE
BLANCO SIGNS OFF WITH A WORLD CUP WARNING

The Times

ENGLAND SLAM FORWARD TO WORLD CUP
LINE TO LINE IN 17 SECONDS

The Guardian

Chapter Seven

VIEWS FROM THE CAPTAINS' TABLE

Compiled by DAVID LLEWELLYN

Paul Thorburn (Wales)

'IT IS AMAZING THAT four years ago many of that team were in the World Cup team we played against and beat 16-3 in the quarter-finals in Brisbane, and really on that performance you would have thought they had a long way to go. But the likes of Wade Dooley, Brian Moore and Peter Winterbottom really worked hard at their game. They thoroughly deserve it. They've been rewarded for a lot of hard work over the last couple of years.

'Fitness has played a big part in it. You just have to take a look at one or two of the guys in the England team now, especially the likes of Dooley and Ackford, compared to three or four years ago. They've obviously done a lot of hard work. They look leaner. They're obviously a lot more conscious of their weight and their body fat and all the technical things that go with training nowadays. They've gelled together well as a side.

'In Wales we have similar fitness regimes. The only thing is perhaps we've got players who aren't really appreciative of the needs or the requirements at the moment. The problem is when you have an unsettled squad, you keep getting new faces and they are not really accustomed to the changes and the requirements. But, having said that, we've got a young squad and hopefully they will know now what lies ahead of them. They've seen with the likes of Dooley that they have progressed enormously with their game and it's only a matter of hard work. And our players have got to do it as well. Then maybe in a year or two we'll be up there at the top.

'Looking at the ages of some of the England players, you'd have thought that the last World Cup would have been their last. But it is now being said that you don't peak physically until you are 34 or 35 and that seems to have been borne out by the England players. But what they have to bear in mind now is that they are going to lose a few of those players over the next couple of years and they might end up in a similar position to the one Wales found themselves in after the seventies, especially in the forwards because that's obviously where England base their game. It's likely that people such as Winterbottom, Dooley, Ackford, Probyn and Rendall will not be there for much longer, so they will have to be looking at their squad and start thinking about bringing on the replacements.

'I am sure the Courage League set-up has helped England enormously – not only the national team but all the junior clubs around them. If your base level is a good standard then obviously the top level is going to be that much higher. We're hoping in Wales that the junior sides such as Dunvant, Felinfoel, etc., will start pushing the top teams and improve fitness levels and the standards. Then maybe we'll have more talent to draw on. At the moment we are picking the Wales team from half a dozen top clubs, and even some of those are not really of the standard you would expect at that level. We are a nation that loves its rugby, but the standards do not reflect that at the moment.

'I sometimes think the success of the seventies worked against Wales. Because we had 15 or so top quality players probably disguised the fact that there was no fresh talent coming through from junior levels. We will never know. It was only at the beginning of the eighties when they lost a load of those players that they began to lose their international credibility. We did win the Triple Crown in '88 and we were unlucky to lose to France in the Grand Slam game. Although it's been a bleak ten years, we have lost a lot of players, which would have hit any of the five nations hard. Wales least of all could afford such losses bearing in mind the dearth of talent. One thing

PAUL THORBURN, NEATH AND WALES

SERGE BLANCO IN ACTION AGAINST SCOTLAND

about international rugby is that it takes time to get used to it and the England players have been around for a long time – Rob Andrew, Richard Hill and so on – and it's only now that they have come into their own.

'I'm a believer that winning is everything. There's no point being silly about it, you play to your strengths, which in England's case is their pack. However, they have got world-class backs. But when games are tight you've got to stick to what you do best. There's no point chucking the ball out willy-nilly just to keep the crowd happy. The fans will be equally pleased with the physical confrontation up front – at least the understanding rugby spectator will be. You can't please everybody in this world. England have been criticised for not running the ball but the point is they've achieved the Grand Slam and won the Five Nations' Championship. New Zealand are winners, but they have been winning a lot longer, so they've got a little more confidence when they open it up.

'I'm sure England will start to throw it around a bit more in the World Cup. They've reached their goal and what they want now is the Cup. You don't get any credit if you play an expansive game but come second. You have to win. Winning is everything and I think England have done well.

'As far as the Cup goes, if they get to the final, which they are quite capable of reaching, it is quite likely that they will come up against Australia, New Zealand or even France. They have other options. The question is, are they confident about using them? You can't neglect your backs for, say, eight games

ROB SAUNDERS SETS UP AN IRISH ATTACK AGAINST ENGLAND IN DUBLIN

and then all of a sudden, when the forwards aren't dominating, expect them to do the business. You've got to bring your backs in at every opportunity to give them confidence with the ball.

'We have a tour to Australia in the summer and we've got to go out there and try to put some kind of platform together for the World Cup. We weren't looking in very good shape before the last one and we surprised a lot of people. So who knows? We've got to start dominating up front. We're aware we've got a lot of hard work to do. It only needs a couple of the other sides to suffer the odd injury to key players – if England lost Dooley or Ackford, for example – then maybe a few cracks would start to appear and we might be able to sneak through.

'This season we had a good game against Ireland. Certain areas of our game with England were all right. When we ran the ball against Scotland, we looked threatening, so it's only a matter of securing possession and retaining it when you are going forward.'

Serge Blanco (France)

'LET'S BE FAIR, we need more experience as a team. Nobody expected we could be here playing a Grand Slam game this season. We have a lot of work to do and I say again that our goal is the World Cup. This game was an important psychological step forward and I told my players before the match that they had to be brave.

'England's win was well deserved. The team that loses the first match of the World Cup [England v New Zealand] will have lost the World Cup. Our first try was great and a great moment for this particular team.'

Rob Saunders (Ireland)

EVEN BEFORE ENGLAND had achieved the Grand Slam, Ireland captain Rob Saunders was critical of their style of play.

As he looked forward to Ireland's match at Lansdowne Road, Saunders said: 'Kicking is, I presume, a very vital part of international rugby, but we'll be instilling discipline into the side.

'Simon Hodgkinson is only a danger when sides give away penalties. He's very lethal with the boot, but if you don't give away penalties then he can't kick them.

'I hope for the sake of the game of rugby that our game against England doesn't turn into a bloody kicking match because that doesn't do any good. Spectators just go home frustrated, which from what I've heard, is how they felt after the Calcutta Cup match.

'The purpose of international rugby is to win, not to entertain, but I don't like the kicking. I prefer an open game. That is the policy at London Irish and of Ireland. We feel we have the talent to run the ball so that's what we do at every opportunity. We can kick when we want to, as we proved against France, but next time out against Wales we showed we can also run the ball.'

But once England had achieved the Grand Slam, Saunders was ready to admit: 'You have to congratulate them. They set out to win the Grand Slam and did it. They have been criticised for not spreading the ball, and New Zealand came in for the same sort of treatment from various quarters, but it works.

'It's not my type of game and anyway we don't have the personnel in Ireland to play their kind of game. If we are to win the Championship and the Grand Slam we will have to do it playing 15-man rugby. But England are very good at what they do.

'There's no doubt they have the backs to spin the ball wide but I can't see them bothering with that. They've obviously decided to tighten the screw after what happened against Scotland last season and it's been effective. I think they'd be crazy to go back to their more expansive game of 1990. They will continue, I am sure, to play this way in the World Cup.

'It will be interesting, that first game between England and New Zealand. It will determine quite a lot. England are good at that forward driving play but they are not exceptional and I think they will find it difficult because other teams are going to work out ways of countering it.'

Chapter Eight

COOKE'S RECIPE FOR SUCCESS

By CHRIS JONES

GEOFF COOKE MADE IT VERY PLAIN where he stood when the England team manager's job landed on his desk in October 1987. 'I want to be very much in charge, a director of operations with assistance from people with particular expertise.' It was the statement of a man determined to stamp his mark on English rugby at international level.

Cooke has achieved that aim and evidence of his importance to the national squad was provided just four days after England had won the Grand Slam for the first time in 11 years. It emerged, much to his embarrassment, that the England team manager had applied to Lancashire and Yorkshire county cricket clubs for their vacant chief executive posts. The subsequent publicity about what he assumed to be confidential applications forced his withdrawal. In the intervening 24 hours leading England players were making their feelings known.

Rob Andrew, the outside half, said: 'Geoff has been vital and almost single-handedly responsible for pulling England together. He has done a wonderful job.'

News of his withdrawal from the job market was comforting, with Brian Moore, the England hooker, stating: 'It is a relief to know his management skills will be available to us in the World Cup.' If one phrase encapsulates Cooke's term in office with England it would be 'man management'. By his actions the former rugby union captain of Cumbria county has given the whole of England management a definite place in the scheme of things. The days of a 'Them and Us' situation existing between selectors and players has been consigned to the history books.

Cooke's ability to throw out the old and impose the new was first seen by the North Division. It was to be the springboard for his elevation to national prominence. 'I wasn't very happy with the system I inherited and we had a poor season with the North,' said Cooke. 'I suggested a tighter management team with the chairman taking a much more direct role, a coach and scope for an assistant coach if we wanted one. We were looking for a structure for the next few years and it worked very well. When it came to picking the team it was much easier for the coach and myself to reach agreement whereas before it was almost a compromise.'

Cooke was offered the England team manager's role when another Northerner, Mike Weston, resigned in the wake of a disappointing World Cup campaign. The date was 16 October 1987, the day the great storm hit Britain. A wind of change was felt in English rugby as Cooke, using the knowledge freely offered by Weston, started to make the team manager's post very much his own. For the Carlisle-born 47-year-old the road to Grand Slam glory in March 1991 involved painful lessons at home and abroad and an introduction to life with the Rugby Football Union committee. A place on that ruling body comes with the job: like it or not!

He did not like the verbal assault aimed at him by RFU committee men on the eve of England's win over Scotland in the middle of the Grand Slam campaign. It resulted from one of the major mistakes of his time in office. After England had beaten Wales in Cardiff for the first time since 1963, Cooke backed the players in their decision not to talk to the media. Instead of receiving the plaudits of a victory dear to every English supporter and RFU committee man, Cooke and the players were hit by a storm of criticism.

Ironically, Cooke was being beaten with his own stick. Open management had been one of the big successes of his tenure, with the team manager always available for interview despite his work schedule. Now he was hammered for not talking to the media and, despite his public acceptance of the mistake, he was reprimanded by the Rugby Football Union. He took the slap on the wrist and normal service was resumed. The RFU committee debated events in Cardiff despite the fact that a reprimand had been issued by Mike Pearey, the RFU President. Cooke discovered he was not supported by some members of the committee who were openly hostile to his continued reign as team manager. Eventually the 50-strong committee agreed to back the President's statement but Cooke never forgot the body blows – even as he savoured the Grand Slam triumph.

When Cooke arrived at England level he was relatively unknown outside the North. His playing career had won him county honours and the captaincy and then secretaryship of the Bradford club. Cooke attended Carlisle Grammar School and studied physical education at St John's College in York. It was logical for the outside half, who also managed to play in every other position behind the scrum, to take up a post as a PE teacher at Temple Moore Grammar School in Leeds. Then there was a career switch that would eventually lead to his current position as chief executive of the British Institute of Sport Coaches. Teaching gave way to a job as PE adviser to Leeds City Council and he was that city's sports development officer when the call came to take over the England team. In

GEOFF COOKE MAKES A POINT

ROGER UTTLEY WANTS HIS FORWARDS TO THINK AHEAD

1975 Cooke had started coaching the Yorkshire county team and enjoyed five years in this role creating an identifiable style. He was made chairman of selectors and that led on to the selection panel for the North Division.

Cooke's first match as part of the North's set-up was memorable. The mighty New Zealand All Blacks were beaten at Otley in 1979 and the division's chairman of selectors at that time was Mike Weston. In 1985 it was Cooke who was given the chairmanship of the North panel and it put his name forward as 'someone to be watched'. When Weston found he could not continue at national level without the assistance of former coach Martin Green, the RFU had to fill the void.

His start as England team manager was hardly impressive with four defeats in the first seven matches but things have considerably improved as Cooke has fine-tuned the system. He has been in charge for 25 matches with 18 victories and often points out that 'only New Zealand have a better record than England in recent seasons'.

Cooke has brought the kind of straight talking to the job that many have found difficult to accept. He does not worry about upsetting those he believes are holding English rugby back through a lack of ambition. His end-of-term reports have made interesting reading and after his England side had hammered Romania in Bucharest in 1989 he wrote: 'Too much of our rugby is based on a safety-first approach with an obsession for the set pieces and kicking as the main tactical planks. Few clubs appear to be working on the development of individual players and equally few produce any back play of note. We must be aware of the potential dangers of fear of failure which still seems to be an inhibiting factor at international level.'

Cooke has continually pointed out that the England management and coaching team cannot be expected to 'coach up' a player in the short time available in squad sessions. Most of the time has to be spent on specifics for the coming international. After missing out on the Grand Slam at Murrayfield in 1990, Cooke took an England squad containing some of the best young talent to Argentina. The aim was to find half a dozen Test players but that proved an unattainable target. At one point he described his players, after a dreadful defeat in Buenos Aires, as 'brain dead'.

His end-of-tour analysis contained a swingeing attack on club coaches. He fumed: 'We have been dismayed that we have had to go back to such basic stuff: where people should stand, where they should run in attack and defence. That is not international coaching. I put this firmly at the door of our coaching system. Day-in-day-out coaching is obviously poor. We have to look very closely at what we are doing. England are a product of what is happening at our clubs, counties and divisions. There are times when I wonder what they are doing at the clubs. We have got to stop being insular and parochial.'

Cooke's hard words sometimes come back to haunt him. Before the Argentine tour started he announced that defeat in either of the Test

ENGLAND EXPECTS . . . TWICKENHAM, MARCH 1991.

BUT SO DOES FRANCE. . . TWICKENHAM, MARCH 1991.

DEAN RICHARDS TRACKS SERGE BLANCO, MARCH 1991.

SIMON HODGKINSON KICKS PAST FRANCK MESNEL AND PHILIPPE SELLA, MARCH 1991.

TEAGUE LEAVES BERBIZIER STRANDED, MARCH 1991.

RICHARD HILL MAKES A BREAK, MARCH 1991.

JEREMY GUSCOTT AND SERGE BLANCO BOTH WANT THIS BALL, MARCH 1991.

PETER WINTERBOTTOM FINDS A SPACE, MARCH 1991.

RORY UNDERWOOD SCORES ENGLAND'S TRY AGAINST FRANCE, MARCH 1991.

PHILIPPE SAINT-ANDRE SCORES FOR FRANCE AT TWICKENHAM, AND FRANCK MESNEL JUMPS FOR JOY, MARCH 1991.

DIDIER CAMBERABERO SCORES THE SECOND FRENCH TRY, AS RORY UNDERWOOD WITNESSES, MARCH 1991.

NIGEL HESLOP RELISHES THE GRAND SLAM CONGRATULATIONS, MARCH 1991.

BLOOD, SWEAT AND JOY FOR MIKE TEAGUE AT THE END OF THE FRENCH MATCH, MARCH 1991.

GRAND SLAM CAPTAIN, WILL CARLING, LEAVES THE FIELD OF HIS GREATEST TRIUMPH, MARCH 1991.

BRIAN MOORE CELEBRATES THE GRAND SLAM IN GRAND PRIX STYLE, MARCH 1991.

matches would be 'a disaster'. That disaster duly happened in the second Test.

Club coaches rounded on their protagonist, claiming he did not visit clubs to find out what was going on and to spread his gospel in person. Quite obviously, there were good guys hit by the verbal broadside along with the bad. However, with this team manager the desire to make England the best rugby team in the world means people will have to get used to the hard talk because it's going to continue. With the 1991 Grand Slam to back up his arguments, Cooke is in a strong position – even against the anti-Cooke faction on the RFU committee.

Chapter Nine

A CAPTAIN OF INDUSTRY
Will Carling

By CHRIS JONES

THE SMILE SAID IT ALL as the crowd carried their hero shoulder high from a Twickenham pitch that had suddenly become a sea of faces. Will Carling, the most successful England captain of all time, had led his team to Grand Slam glory. Cardiff 1989, Murrayfield 1990, Buenos Aires 1990; now all forgotten.

Those capital cities had hosted great English disasters as Carling's team failed to live up to the pre-match predictions. Twickenham 1991 on a wet afternoon in March erased the bad memories and killed the belief that this was the best England team never to have won anything. Carling knew the Grand Slam was England's before the final whistle. 'You get a feel for a game and, despite the tries the French scored I knew we were going to win,' said the 25-year-old. Of course, Carling was right and the absolute joy of getting it right was there for everyone to see as the crowd chaired him towards the dressing-room and a champagne celebration with the rest of the England team.

For Carling the Grand Slam provided a storybook climax to the rugby dream of a six-year-old who wanted to grow up and be an England player. The kid grew up to be an England captain with a record of 13 wins in 17 internationals. It is indelible evidence that Geoff Cooke, the England team manager, had been right all along when he shocked English rugby in 1988. A new captain had to be found to take on Australia that November and Cooke announced the name of William David Charles Carling to the waiting press corps. While it wasn't quite a case of 'Will who?', he was still a novice international. At 22 he was also the baby of the team.

Up to that point Carling's main pressure had been to answer the many letters from an army of female admirers. Now, the band that would be following him around would carry pens for quotes not autographs and cameras for broadcast purposes not snap shots. Carling made the right kind of start by captaining England to victory over Australia. Simon Halliday, his great friend and fellow centre, scored a try which Carling just about saw. He had been pole-axed passing to Halliday and a helpful team-mate lifted Carling's head from the turf so he could witness the try. When he was eventually ordered off by the England doctor, the crowd rose as a man to cheer.

It was obvious that English rugby had managed to appoint a young man who would broaden the appeal and exposure of the game. The focus of attention since 1988 has been on Carling, manifesting itself in the form of magazine cover pictures, appearances on *Wogan* and endless feature material. His waist measurement, tailoring problems and inability to sing any dirty rugby songs have become public knowledge.

All this attention would have been meaningless if the Harlequins centre had failed to perform at a consistently high level in the rarified atmosphere of international rugby. In fact, Carling is a genuinely world-class centre possessing speed and strength allied to a tactical brain eager to absorb new ideas. He has become the recognised face of English rugby and people seem either to like him or loathe him because of this fact of life. As Carling said when asked about his influence as captain in 1988: 'Before, no one ever dared say anything for fear of being kicked out. Perhaps I am a bit more arrogant, self-confident if you like, but I think the management respect that I am my own man and I'll speak my own mind.'

Cooke created the right atmosphere for Carling's 'new England' to flourish and eradicated the divisive elements that had been present in previous squads. Lines of communication (a favourite theme of Carling's) were installed and defined while coach Roger Uttley brought a forthright approach that sat well between Carling and Cooke. Now all they had to do was win something.

For Carling one of the most important tasks was to prove that England rugby teams could win when made favourites. It was obvious that Carling's team had real class and potential but an inability to rise to the ultimate challenge labelled England underachievers. It was a tag first earned by the teams that followed the 1980 Grand Slam side and was to remain until Carling's men triumphed 11 years later. As he said: 'I think English sides have always had the potential to win. People always say that about England. But mostly, the players have never had the confidence. They think if they try something and it goes wrong they will be dropped.'

To counter this feeling of instability, Carling realised he had to try and turn the England squad into an extension of a club side. He wanted his players to feel as if they were really part of something special rather than a collection of 'the best' thrown together at certain points in the season to save the country's rugby honour. It was all very psychological and very much up his street. Carling was schooled at Sedbergh and moved on to Durham University to study psychology on an Army Scholarship. It would prove to be a valuable grounding.

WILL CARLING: 'PERHAPS I'M A BIT MORE ARROGANT, SELF-CONFIDENT IF YOU LIKE, BUT I THINK THE MANAGEMENT RESPECT THE FACT THAT I AM MY OWN MAN AND I'LL SPEAK MY OWN MIND'

All his views on teamwork and the collective effort would have remained unused if Carling's rugby career had not flourished with his education. Sedbergh brought him the captaincy of England Schools in 1984 and when he arrived at Durham he was moved to fullback. He was picked as a centre by the North who were, at that time, managed by Geoff Cooke. He made an immediate impact and international rugby quickly followed plus the role of inside centre.

It appeared that Carling was set for a career in the Army, following in the footsteps of his father and brother. However, the Army, much to their subsequent regret, remained inflexible when Carling presented his rugby programme and length of time off. A parting of the ways was the only answer and after a short spell with Mobil Oil he set up Inspirational Horizons, based near Piccadilly Circus, offering companies motivational help with their staff. Carling drives a top-of-the-range Mercedes and is very much the young businessman.

Back on the rugby pitch, though, Carling was discovering that England were still losing the big ones. A missed Championship in 1989, Grand Slam defeat in 1990 and then a shared series with Argentina gave the doubters plenty of ammunition. Even his captaincy was given a working over in the aftermath of the Grand Slam defeat by Scotland. Claims that he did not have complete control over events during the match abounded. His insistence on collective responsibility left him open to sustained flak and Carling made a conscious decision to change his style. When penalties were awarded to England during their 1990 tour of Argentina it was Carling who raced forward to take hold of the ball. It was a gesture to those on the sidelines who said he had not been the dominant figure at Murrayfield and the new style continued throughout the Five Nations' Championship.

There was another altogether different theme running through the Championship as well and it proved to be a considerable irritant to Carling and his team. The International Rugby Board's relaxation of the game's amateur laws allowed players to make money from non-rugby related activities. However, that produced so many grey areas it was a potential minefield. Carling and his men wandered into the danger zone and copped a collective face full of shrapnel in the process. The anti-players backlash eventually led to a highly public decision to part company with the agents hired to make the England squad money.

The real problem stemmed from a collective decision, supported by Cooke, not to talk to the media in Cardiff after Wales had been beaten on their own pitch for the first time in 28 years. The press and public reaction was hostile and the victory was buried under claim and counter-claim about the real reason for the row. Was it a £5,000 fee for television interviews? The players said 'No'.

The decision to sever Player Vision, the company set up by the players, from the Willis organisation was aimed at improving their image and concentrating on the job in hand: winning the Grand Slam. Carling cut down the number of pre-match television interviews and press features in a personal effort to establish the idea that this was a team effort for glory, not an ego trip on the back of 14 mates.

Through the bad times this season Carling has enjoyed the full support of the management team and, more importantly, the England squad. He spends hours on the telephone checking with fellow England players on matters that cover the whole range of rugby and private life. Flowers for a player's wife who has just given birth is a small example of the captain's attitude and support for his team. Throw in charity work for the causes he supports (the number asking for something is amazing) and suddenly the arrogant image starts to melt. He enjoys taking a break from the pressures of his position by returning to the family home where he can really relax.

The bottom line is that Carling loves playing rugby union. He has turned down £1 million to become a rugby league star and is adamant that it is an option he will never take. He explained: 'I have been offered a lot of money but I have been playing rugby union since I was six and I love it. The way I see it, if someone were to pay me to play rugby they would have a hold on me and I don't want that. I play for fun and I play when and where I want to. That is one of the beauties of the game.'

With the Grand Slam won and a real chance for England in the 1991 World Cup, the game is looking particularly good for Carling at the moment. 'It is difficult to describe but it is lovely to be part of a successful set-up. It would take a far more eloquent person than me to put it into words.'

Chapter Ten

TWIN PEAKS AND HIGH KICKS

Dooley, Ackford and Hodgkinson

By JOHN REASON

WHEN YOU CONSIDER THAT ENGLAND built most of their strategy for the 1991 season on the sheer physical presence of Wade Dooley and Paul Ackford in the line-out, and on the goal-kicking of Simon Hodgkinson at fullback, a truly remarkable statistic emerged from the match in which England beat France for both the International Championship and the Grand Slam.

In the whole of that match at Twickenham, Dooley – all six foot eight inches of him – did not win one ball at the line-out. His take, as the American President George Bush might have said, was zilch. Zero. Zed. It was the first whitewash in Dooley's entire career as an international line-out jumper. In his early days, Dooley had his troubles against Bob Norster, of Wales, but even Norster never did anything like that to him.

Damian Cronin, who has worn the number five shirt for Scotland this season, might have found that difficult to believe. As I have pointed out before, it is not often that you see someone finish 14th in a two-man contest, but that was what happened to Cronin in the Calcutta Cup match against Dooley and England.

The man who delivered the line-out goods for England against France was Ackford. Those goods were nowhere near as plentiful for England as they had been against Ireland and Scotland, but they were crucial nonetheless, particularly when France, even in the soaking rain, were threatening to produce another mighty bound to break free of their shackles and win the match.

France had already produced one of those in the first ten minutes of the game to score a try which, if the BBC's camera direction had been a whole lot better, might even have given some airtime competition to Gareth Edwards's famous try for the Barbarians against the New Zealand All Blacks at Cardiff in 1973.

That was why the four clean takes that Ackford made at the end of the match were so important, as were the two ricochets also picked up by Dean Richards. The only way to stop the French backs was to stop them getting the ball. Even so, it will remain for ever a matter of wonder and amazement that out of 40 throws into the line-out in a match as important as that, Dooley did not win one of them. This reinforces the theory that Dooley and Ackford are absolutely essential to each other, and that this is why they took so long to emerge as international players.

Back in 1978, when he was still only 20 years old, Ackford had played for South and South-West counties against New Zealand at Bristol, and at the end of their tour the All Blacks rated him as the most promising forward they had played against. It took Ackford exactly ten more years to fulfil that promise and win his first cap for England and, in that time, he learned just what a tough old life it can be when you are playing as a lock forward in first-class rugby. In that time, too, his rating among the leading practitioners in his trade dropped so far through the floor that he must have felt like giving up the game. One day, on a flight back from Romania, I happened to be sitting next to a former first-class lock forward who had been among those who had worked out how to cope with the young Ackford. 'How did you play him?' I asked.

My companion, a Londoner born and bred, with more than a trace of the local dialect in his accent, thought for a few moments, wondering whether to tell me the truth, and then smiled a distant and affectionate smile in memory of happy times past. 'I used to 'it 'im, didn't I? We all did. Paul's trouble was 'e was much too nice a lad. Read a lot of books, and that sort of stuff. A schoolmaster. Went to Cambridge. But you could put 'im off 'is game. It was a pity, really, because 'e could 'ave been a good player, if somebody 'ad got 'old of 'im. Well, that's obvious, innit, because 'e *is* a good player now. Perhaps becoming a copper 'as 'elped 'im.'

Ackford nearly disappeared from the game in those years he spent in academia. It was not until the London Division picked him up in 1988, after he had joined both the fuzz and the Harlequins, that his rocket to the stars was picked up off the ground and reignited.

At that stage, at what seemed to be the dog-end of his playing career, Ackford was still a middle jumper, as he always had been. That was where he played, in partnership with Neil Edwards, when he played for London against the touring Australians at Twickenham, but three weeks after that match, when he won his first cap for England, Ackford played as a front jumper in partnership with Dooley.

Ackford's performance in that game against Australia, which England won well, earned the unqualified admiration of the England loosehead prop Paul Rendall who, as he puts it, has been 'looking after' line-out jumpers for very many years. 'That game made him,' says Rendall. 'Within a year, he was world class. At the age of 30! I could remember him when he was so raw you couldn't believe it.'

Within that year that Rendall talks about, Ackford had become just as potent a force in the Lions Test team in Australia. Before the tour, he was just as diffident and as unassertive as he had always been; just as quick to explain why players like Ireland's Donal Lenihan were so much better qualified than 31-year-old England debutante-like giant, and even more verily a late and slow developer.

Dooley was just the same. Like Ackford, he is also a policeman. The difference is that Dooley always has been.

Richard Greenwood, who became England's coach, recalls that when he was playing a minor club match in Lancashire 12 years ago, he followed his usual practice of nosing round the corridors outside the dressing-rooms before the match to spy out the land and bumped into this colossus. Greenwood remembers that his forehead collided with Dooley at a point just below the breast bone.

'"Christ," I thought,' said Greenwood, '"What have we got here?" Fortunately when we played the game, Wade gave us all sorts of problems for 20 minutes, and then he disappeared. But anyone who comes into the ring at that sort of size is not the sort of lad you forget easily. I could see that the talent was there, but there didn't seem to be much in the way of inclination. He didn't have the self-belief.

'It was a slow-dawning process, too. Policemen have a pretty comfortable existence, and I don't suppose it occurred to Wade for even a minute that he might have some pretensions to playing for someone other than his local police side in Lancashire or for Preston Grasshoppers.

'But there then occurred a series of accidents. Steve Bainbridge got sent off. Bob Kimmins got injured. So, suddenly, Wade got a game for Lancashire, and I managed to persuade him that sergeant jumps was not the name of an officer in a nearby force. Up to then, Wade had never had to jump at all. He just stood there and people lobbed the ball at him. That's all that was necessary. But shortly after that, Preston Grasshoppers played Waterloo in the Lancashire Cup and actually beat them.

'Round about that time, Wade was picked as a replacement for the North against one of those All Black teams that were turning up every five minutes. There he was, sitting on the bench, when someone on the field sliced a wild kick to glory. It looked as if it was going out of the ground, but Wade just stood up and caught it. He must be the only player who ever really made enough of an impact to catch the eye of the selectors while he was actually sitting on the bench.'

Eventually, Greenwood managed to persuade the England selectors that Preston Grasshoppers really did have a very large lump of very raw material that was worth developing, and Greenwood admits that playing for the PG's did not help his cause. 'Lancashire is not an easy place to get on in. There is a very strict protocol in the social ranking of clubs and Grasshoppers were so far below the salt you would have needed a telescope to see them.'

One of Greenwood's earliest and biggest problems with his protégé was to stop him smiling. 'Wade really is the epitome of the gentle giant. I could not even get him to glower, never mind raise a fist in anger. This was one of the reasons why, when he started to play international rugby, he always had so much trouble with Bob Norster.

'Bob was a most knowledgeable jumper, and he was an athlete too. He knew all the tricks of the trade. When to take a short ball. When to move into it. When to move away from it. When to give his man a nudge. When to give his man something a little stronger. He gave Wade no end of problems.

'That was why the bust-up in Cardiff, which got Wade suspended, was so ridiculous. England went down there determined that they were fed up with being knocked about, and they were going to do something about it. So they did. Right on cue. The trouble was that when Wade eventually arrived to make his contribution to the fight, the matter was bordering on the posthumous.

'What Wade did, and did very, very late, was make a gesture of obedience, as opposed to malice. I know that is difficult to sustain in a court of law, or even after a rerun of the video, but anyone knowing the man would have been far more forgiving. The great thing is that he came back from that and went on from that, and I am sure that he owes most of the success he has enjoyed since to his partnership with Paul Ackford. They have both been much better players as a consequence of that partnership. It really is one of those situations where the whole is greater than the sum of the parts.

'The great thing is that Dooley never lets you down. He doesn't have many masterpiece games, although he did have one in his first match against France and he had another against Damian Cronin this season, but he never has a catastrophe. Even in the last match against France this season, where the ball eluded him, he managed to inhibit the opposition just by standing there. He even managed to inhibit their selection, by persuading them to make a couple of purely negative selections, aimed at simply stopping England, rather than make two positive selections, aimed at starting France. It was as well for England that he did.

'Wade has made an enormous improvement in his scrummaging, too. When I first played behind him as a number eight, his backside was so high in the air I very nearly needed a stepladder to make contact with it. These days Wade Dooley is a very capable all-round forward. The tackle he made on Serge Blanco at the end of the match against France was a case in point.

'The point about Wade is that even if he doesn't deliver, he is a perceived threat. The opposition just can't ignore him. That makes life easier for everyone else – even for a player as great as Dean Richards. Only Bob Norster has ever rumbled Wade Dooley. I think Nigel Horton would have done, too, because he was the original line-out academic, the original psycher-out, the

ACKFORD AND DOOLEY CONSULT WITH ENGLAND CAPTAIN CARLING

WADE DOOLEY AND PAUL ACKFORD

original schemer, the original deviser of subtleties. But then Nigel was on our side, or he would have been if England had picked him as often as they should have done.'

The same observation might have been made about England's treatment of Simon Hodgkinson. When he came on to the field at Leicester as a young replacement for the injured Les Cusworth against the Australians in November 1984, Hodgkinson was a confident young fly half. He did not seem in the least abashed, even though the Australians went on to complete a Grand Slam of victories against England, Scotland, Ireland and Wales on their tour.

They were playing the Midlands Division that night and they were having their problems. Their hooker, Mark McBain, was sent off the field by referee Winston Jones along with Peter Wheeler of the Midlands, and the whole game was turning out to be far too much of a close-run thing for the liking of the Australians.

Then Cusworth was injured, but if the Wallabies thought that the loss of such an experienced player would make the Midlands' task that much more difficult, they were soon disillusioned. No sooner had the young Hodgkinson arrived than he dropped a goal and the Australians were glad to scrape home 21–18.

Hodgkinson's confidence and the authority of his kicking did not surprise Alan Davies, his coach at Nottingham. 'Simon has always looked pale and frail,' he says, 'but even as a teenager, he always had the ability to kick a ball from one end of the field to the other as if he was not really trying. It's all to do with timing. He has never been a whacker. He just strokes the ball and it goes.'

There are those who believe that if Hodgkinson had gone on playing fly half he would have been able to do for England exactly what Grant Fox has done for New Zealand because they are almost identical in their abilities. Both are footballers. Both have good hands. Both are exceptional kickers. Both have a vision of the game. Both are capable of the very occasional, but nevertheless insidious, run. Neither would ever qualify to play as a blocker in American football.

But in international rugby, cookies crumble in different ways, and Simon Hodgkinson perceived that if he was to play for England, he would have to do it as a makeshift fullback who could earn his keep by kicking goals. He knew he would never be able to come scouring through from the back like John Gallagher of New Zealand. He knew he would never have the lissom pace or the genius of improvisation of a player like Serge Blanco of France. He knew he would never have the sheer power of a fullback like Gavin Hastings of Scotland. But he knew he could kick goals, and he knew he could keep out of trouble to a much greater extent than many knowledgeable sceptics believed.

A lot of opponents have aimed high kicks at Hodgkinson with the idea of bombing him to destruction. No one has yet succeeded. As often as not, the reply has been a safe catch and an irritatingly big touch-finder in return, or a carefully considered little run back followed by a raking, rolling kick which seems to potter down the field for ever before expiring into touch at a point usually well past the point where the would-be bomber launched his missile. Hodgkinson has been a great frown-maker among opponents in his time.

The frowns he caused among the Romanians when he began his international career in Bucharest in 1989 were so deep that they almost became a psychiatric concern. It was a blazing hot day, but Hodgkinson was as cool and collected as ever. Whether he was cool or not, I do not know, but he certainly collected. He kicked eight conversions and a penalty goal in England's victory by 58 points to three. That gave him 19 points and a lasting affection for the Adidas chrome leather ball with the black ends.

Since then he has accumulated points in international rugby almost as fast as Fox. The sceptics thought that could not last, particularly after he had missed a sitter of a kick against Argentina in Buenos Aires last summer.

That cost England the match – their first ever defeat by Argentina – and the theory was that Hodgkinson's confidence would be badly shaken for the International Championship in 1991, especially as England's Five Nations' campaign was due to start against Wales in Cardiff.

England had not won in Cardiff since 1963 and with a real gun goal-kicker like Paul Thorburn wielding the three-shooter at the other end, the feeling was that the wraith from Nottingham might be shot to pieces when the two of them met in Westgate Street. Not a bit of it. Thorburn was the man who finished the match with his toes pointing to the sky. Hodgkinson broke a world record by kicking seven penalty goals and quietly blew the smoke out of his barrel before edging through the door.

He kicked Scotland to death as well, and by the time he had come to terms with an unfamiliar ball against Ireland, he had scored 46 points in three matches and had broken Dusty Hare's England record of 44 points in a season in the Five Nations' Championship.

The point was or, rather, the points were, that Simon Hodgkinson had the Grand Slam match against France to break Jean-Patrick Lescarboura's record of 54 points.

The question was: could England contain the brilliant French backs? The answer was: no, they couldn't, but although England lost the try count Simon Hodgkinson won the goal-kicking count 14–7. That gave England the Grand Slam. It also gave Hodgkinson Lescarboura's record and an average of more than 14 points a match in international rugby. Not bad for a makeshift fullback.

Chapter Eleven

SHARED JOURNEY
Andrew and Underwood

By MICHAEL CALVIN

IT WAS THE STUFF of first-form fantasy. Rob Andrew and Rory Underwood, friends from the age of 11, bobbed around on the human sea that lapped up against Twickenham's West Stand, savouring the realisation they had helped England win the Grand Slam.

Someone in the celebratory scrum of supporters had jammed an England cap on Underwood's head. He leant back on willing hands, ignored the rain on his face, and bellowed out a chorus of *Swing Low, Sweet Chariot*, one of international sport's more unlikely signature tunes.

Andrew, a matter of feet away, joined in the community singing. He was pushed forward, on an anonymous fan's shoulder, by the force of congratulatory slaps on the back, but regained his balance and thrust both fists skyward in triumph.

A shared journey, that had begun with a 6–4 victory for the Under-12s of Barnard Castle School over Durham School, their traditional local rivals, had reached a copybook conclusion with the 21–19 win over France that was a vivid showcase for their sport.

Underwood marked his arrival, alongside Tony Neary, as England's most capped player with his 27th try in 43 international appearances. Andrew reinforced his individual records by scoring his tenth drop goal in his 36th match as England's outside half, ample reward for his persistence. Their reactions to the most enduring achievement of their sporting lives reflected their distinctive characters.

Underwood, unfailingly polite but reticent when invited to indulge in public self-analysis, sipped lemonade and radiated a quiet sense of satisfaction. He quickly readjusted his sights to the challenge of the World Cup, which England players see in the distance, rather like mountaineers glimpsing the peak of Everest through a veil of Himalayan cloud.

'We're in the record books now,' he reflected. 'No one can take the Grand

Slam away from us. But we have always seen it as a big stepping-stone to the World Cup. I'm not saying we'll win it, but I wouldn't be devoting all this time to it if I didn't think we had a real chance.'

Andrew, at just turned 28, four months older but equally thoughtful, was more emotional about the self-justification offered by the Five Nations' title. He has been hardened by the criticism that accompanied his being dropped twice in the initial stages of his international career, and shaped by the sacrifice of time and effort.

'Flippantly, you say this is a dream, but it is more than that,' he said, signing autographs as he stood, with his family, around a table in Twickenham's Rose Room. 'Seven years' hard work and heartache has gone into this. It is almost impossible to put into words what it all means. There are times when you wonder if it's worth going on. The pressure you are under, the pressure you place on yourself, is just incredible. I can't imagine how I would have coped had we lost. It doesn't bear thinking about.'

His maturity, evident in the understanding forged with scrum half Richard Hill, another relative veteran, was one of the key elements in England's season. As befitting his status as natural deputy to captain Will Carling, he was an authoritative figure both on and off the field.

The predatory Underwood, too, made a predictably crucial contribution. Since Carling cited his decisive try against Ireland at Lansdowne Road as a turning point, even the notoriously modest Leicester wing was forced to admit, 'Looking back, me bringing us back into that game was very, very important.'

Typically, he was operating on instinct at the time, forcing himself to concentrate on reaching a hastily selected spot in the corner after, without conscious thought, transferring the ball to the technically correct hand. In such circumstances, where momentary indecision can be calamitous, he summons instant pace, and seeks to turn the tacklers' momentum to his advantage.

Andrew reflected: 'Rory has always been able to get the ball down in seemingly impossible situations. His try against Ireland was by no means impossible, but he ought not to have scored and it is not as simple as blaming the Irish defence.'

Mike Slemen, the England B coach who until Underwood's emergence was his country's most capped wing with 31, agreed. 'It was a great try because there was absolutely nothing on,' he said. 'At that stage England were struggling. But it was a bit of brilliance from a talented individual and that is what the game is about at that level. It was a typical Rory try. The reason he scores so heavily is his awareness of where the line is. He gets the ball down where all around him is mayhem.'

Geoff Cooke, England's manager, recognised immediately the potential of Underwood's tactical nous when he first saw him play for Durham Colts. The reputation the rapidly developing schoolboy had established in his final

ROB ANDREW: 'SEVEN YEARS HARD WORK AND HEARTACHE HAS GONE INTO THIS'

term at Barnard Castle, when he scored 39 tries in 13 matches, was fully borne out.

Underwood is recognised by contemporaries such as Ieuan Evans, the Wales wing, and Scotland's Tony Stanger as a matchless finisher. Cooke argues: 'I have seen him score tries – a lot of great tries – which no one in the world would have got.'

A natural sportsman who was drawn into rugby 'like most people, simply because it was played at school', Underwood joined the RAF as a jet pilot while Andrew went on to captain Cambridge University in both cricket and rugby.

He was first capped against Ireland in February 1984, but, starved of adequate service and susceptible to occasional lapses in concentration, scored only four tries in his first 22 games. The challenge to his supremacy, implicit in his obligation to move to the right wing to accommodate the injury-prone Chris Oti in 1989, proved to be a profound source of inspiration.

'I think for the first time he felt under real pressure,' reflected Andrew. 'There has been a big change in Rory over the past couple of years. He never used to be that worried about making a wider contribution, but Geoff Cooke brought him out of himself.'

Underwood appreciates the logic of his friend's argument. 'Up until three or four years ago we turned up, threw the ball about a bit, went out and played,' he said. 'Now every aspect of our game is dismembered, talked about, and put back together. If anything, over the seven years I have been in the England team, I have become less specialised. Of course, I'm aware of my responsibilities, but it is not just a case of "get the ball and score". I have been encouraged to develop other attributes. I'm more mature as a person. I'd like to think I'm more conscious of my experience benefiting others.'

Carling, whose strength as a captain is his recognition of the importance of the individual opinion within a closely knit squad, admits he values Underwood's advice. 'Rory thinks deeply about the game,' he explained. 'He is quiet and thoughtful, but immensely experienced.' The same can be said of Andrew, who learned, the hard way, that attack is the best form of self-defence in the exposed world of international sport.

He made his England debut against Romania in 1985 but it was not until the Lions tour of Australia in 1989, when he established himself as a world-class outside half after flying out as replacement for Ireland's Paul Deans, that he silenced the shrill doubts of his persistent critics.

'All internationals are blown up out of all proportion these days, and the first time you are publicly criticised it hits you hard,' he admitted. 'It wounds you because you don't really understand it. It is a fact of life, but a harsh fact to come to terms with.'

Consequently, he was able to put the simplistic sniping about England's pragmatic approach to the 1991 season into its proper perspective. Though a forceful advocate for change in rugby's guidelines on amateurism, he

RORY UNDERWOOD: 'WE'RE IN THE RECORD BOOKS NOW. NO ONE CAN TAKE THE GRAND SLAM AWAY FROM US'

was sufficiently open-minded to accept that ordinary working life had its merits.

International sport is notorious for distorting the values of the personalities it creates and, as a highly regarded chartered surveyor, he appreciated, more than ever, the change in tempo of travelling to his London office on a 7.30 a.m. tube. It reminded him of the realities of everyday life.

However, in World Cup year, it hardly proved an effective shield from the pressures of what has become as suffocating an existence as that endured by any high-profile professional athlete. Both men admit, with a revealing bashfulness, they have become recognisable figures even though, in Underwood's words, they consider themselves merely to be 'working members of the public who happen to play international rugby'.

Underwood, like Andrew, has a young family to support. Though playing for the RAF, the equivalent of Gary Lineker turning out for the staff side of Tottenham Hotspur PLC in the local Sunday League, underlines his equitable nature, he identifies with his friend's dilemma.

He has time on his side and still harbours the hope he will appear in the same England side as his younger brother, Tony, the B international who plays on the opposite wing at Leicester and toured Argentina with the full squad last summer, when he concentrated on RAF duties.

However, he admitted, 'I'm finding it harder, coping with the time away, the time travelling. That time is precious when you are married with a child. When there is a two or three-hour slot in your day, filled with rugby, you sometimes think, "Is there something else I could be doing?" A family puts things into perspective – it is far more important than rugby. It is all a balancing act. I'll know when I've reached the stage where I've had enough. I'm not someone who looks that far forward, but I've not yet lost that basic sense of satisfaction from playing the game. When you've scored, and the crowd are yelling, that's what rugby is all about.'

The pair will decide their futures after the World Cup, where the spotlight threatens to burn with unprecedented intensity. It is hard to shake off the suspicion that their decisions will be similar.

There is an obvious temptation for Underwood to underscore his name in the record books. Barring unforeseen circumstances, he will become England's most capped player in this summer's Test match in Fiji.

'People at work talk to me about such things but, to be honest, I don't like to think about creating records,' he reflected. 'I've had my so-so games for England. I might get dropped, and that will be that. There is too much to think about, during a game, to consider statistics, but I'd be a liar if I told you I didn't realise the records were there. I had a great sense of pride at Twickenham, but it's just that I try to maintain this sense of reality.'

Andrew dutifully placed such sentiments into the context of his friend's character. 'When you analyse what Rory has achieved in terms of caps and tries he is phenomenal,' he said. 'But he doesn't make a big deal about it, he just gets on with life. That's his way of coming to terms with it all. I don't know how long we'll all keep going for. Everyone is asking himself that same question, and a lot will depend on what happens in the World Cup. It will be interesting to see what happens if, say, half the side calls it a day. That's what happened with the last Grand Slam squad which, like ours, was very settled. It took England five or six years to recover, and that type of situation presents its own challenge.'

Honourable retirement is, undoubtedly, an attractive option. But, whatever decisions they reach in the months to come, Underwood and Andrew have one important thing in common. They have grown up to be winners.

Chapter Twelve

BACK-ROW CONNECTION
Winterbottom, Teague and Richards

By JAMIE SALMON

THERE IS ABSOLUTELY NO DOUBT that the one area in which England totally dominated throughout the Championship was in the back row. Collectively and individually, Winterbottom, Teague and Richards enjoyed outstanding seasons. They were side by side in every game and the back-row moves enabled England to put enormous pressure on the opposition.

For Peter Winterbottom, now 30, the wait for a Grand Slam has been long and hard. Capped in 1982, he has now collected 42 caps and would have already reached 50 but for some inconsistency of the selectors over the years. He is held in enormous respect by team-mates and opponents for his sheer determination and attitude to the game. His early years as an international were marked by his ferocious tackling and support play. A criticism of his handling skills was justified, but he spent hours on the training field to remedy the fault and can now give and take a pass like a centre three-quarter. He is an uncomplicated person who does not believe in grey areas on any issue and feels that guts and heart can beat most things.

Now working in the City of London as a Eurobond dealer, he is experiencing a larger life. No more is he left on the farm outside Leeds where his childhood was spent. He knows that time is running out for him as an open-side flanker, but will no doubt continue to play club rugby rather than finish altogether. He knows that nothing could have been possible without the help of his club colleagues, first at Headingly, then Harlequins. He has never sought the limelight, always preferring the company of his mates. I played for both club and country with him and you could not wish to have a better bloke on your side. The only thing that has ever amazed me about him is that he never wears a mouthguard. He tried one once, did not like it, and has not bothered since. I dare say that his dental bill will be rather expensive when he eventually decides to hang up the boots.

In 1980, when England won the Grand Slam, Tony Neary was the open-side flanker and won a record 43 caps. Like Winterbottom, he should have reached 50 but for the selectors. Quicker than Winterbottom, Neary was probably a more creative player who anticipated the opposition moves in advance. The one basic similarity of the two was that each has incredible stamina enabling them to last the full 80 minutes at the same pace.

Mike Teague's career has been up and down to say the least. First capped as a number eight in 1985, it took the Lions tour of Australia in 1989 to put his name on the map. Even this season he was dropped for the match against Argentina for John Hall but, without drama, has bounced back and scored two key tries in the Championship.

Teague's nickname amongst the England boys is 'Iron Mike' because of his incredible upper body frame, which looks more suited to the boxing ring. This power gives Teague the force to drive the opposition backwards and get over the gain line to keep his colleagues going forward.

Teague has been brought up in one of rugby's most famous clubs. West Country born, he is immensely proud of Gloucester and all that it represents. Like Winterbottom, he is the wrong side of 30 and next season will probably be his last international one. Off the field, he is rather quiet and almost shy with a dry sense of humour. One of his great moments in the Championship was to score the only try at Cardiff. Two years before, he had left the field after a minute of play through injury.

The England coach, Roger Uttley, has no doubt had a big influence on Teague. Uttley played blindside flanker in 1980 and was similar to Teague in that his driving play was difficult to stop. Ironically, both played for their clubs at number eight and can be justifiably called 'hard men'. Neither is afraid to tread where few others would dare and they no doubt share a mutual respect.

Who could forget, when England played Wales in 1980, Uttley leaving the field with blood pouring from his face. The scars are still visible today so when Uttley asks Teague to do something, Teague knows that his coach has done it all himself.

Dean Richards can arguably be acclaimed as the world's best number eight and one of England's all-time greats. Totally unorthodox, he is the colossus of the team. Shirt hanging out, socks down and one of the worst running styles ever seen are the hallmarks of Richards. When England ran out for the decider against France, Richards was last out of the tunnel. Slowly trotting across the pitch, he remained totally cool and composed before proceeding to play a marvellous game.

Despite being only 27, he has suggested that next year may well be his last as he does not really enjoy the level of commitment now required of international players. He does not see rugby as anything more than a hobby

PETER WINTERBOTTOM: GUTS AND HEART

MIKE TEAGUE: 'IRON MIKE' TO HIS TEAM-MATES

and, much as he likes winning, there are other things in life to worry about. Furthermore, he hates training.

On the field, his presence is immense. He has an incredible ability to be in the right place at the right time and possesses enormous upper body strength, which enables him to stay on his feet long enough so the support can arrive. Though not the tallest of number eights, he still wins his share of line-out ball and drives the team forwards, so presenting Richard Hill with the clean ball to move away.

Despite his appearance, Richards has one of the most astute rugby brains and knows when and why to change tactics. In Ireland he controlled the last quarter of the game, advising Hill of all the options required. He kept England going forward, thus ensuring that they were awarded the put-ins to the scrum.

At his club, he is most relaxed. He enjoys the club scene and enjoys the whole set-up of Leicester. He respects the club for its marvellous traditions and the loyal crowd that follows the team everywhere. Four days after the Ireland game, he played for Leicester in a match of no significance when his England colleagues would have had their feet up. I dare say that, if he does retire from international rugby next year, he will play on with Leicester, enjoying the fact that virtually every weekend after Christmas he will not be on the M1 to London for another England squad session. He is not in the least bit interested in records or the number of caps he could possibly attain.

In 1980, John Scott was England's number eight, enjoying a dominating season with Neary and Uttley. He was probably a better line-out forward than Richards and certainly looked more of an athlete and ball player. He had a great understanding with his scrum half, Steve Smith, as they often disappeared down the blind side together. Like Richards, he had an astute rugby brain – hence his elevation to the captaincy some years later – and he now manages Cardiff. He would have learnt a lot from the senior pros around him, a list including Beaumont, Cotton and Wheeler.

The current back row probably does have a weakness in that none of them are particularly quick. Against New Zealand and their back row, which includes Michael Jones and Mike Brewer, they will most certainly be up against it in the opening encounter of the World Cup this October. To counter that, their sheer physical presence will ensure that the All Blacks will have plenty of tackling to do and it promises to be one of the great battles. Of the England trio, only Richards has yet to play the All Blacks. Winterbottom played for the Lions against them in '83 and Teague for England in '85, which is the last time the two teams met. Both parties will no doubt pay each other every respect.

During this season, however, the England back row reigned supreme. The power of their performances has been a pleasure to watch, as has their sheer determination to meet any crisis and defend their try line with all they have.

DEAN RICHARDS, ARGUABLY THE WORLD'S BEST NUMBER EIGHT

It will have also given great pleasure to Uttley, who has full knowledge of the importance of the back row. Three good players don't necessarily make a good back row. They have to get together and understand each other's strengths and weaknesses so they can complement each other in every department of the game.

They have to enjoy each other's company off the field and take pride in their collective performance. Every so often, you will see them talking together during a game, encouraging themselves to greater heights and further dominance upon the opposition. On the practice field, back row moves that launch an attack have to be rehearsed to perfection.

People always talk of the front-row club, but it applies just as much to the back row. The first drink of the evening is always shared together and the second is with the opposing back row. Thus friendship is extended.

The back row is physically demanding and dangerous. Time and time again, their bodies are subject to cuts and bruises. I remember Winterbottom receiving stitches above the eye one day and being asked how it was. 'Just the four,' was the reply and off he went.

Winterbottom, Teague and Richards have undoubtedly been England's outstanding performers in the Championship along with Rob Andrew. After each game, the press and public heaped praise upon the manner of their achievements. Basically, they are three very down-to-earth Englishmen. They do, however, have an enormous passion in their own and their team's performance. And they decided that this was going to be the year that English fans would not forget.

Chapter Thirteen

FRONT-ROW UNION
Probyn, Moore and Leonard

By BRENDAN GALLAGHER

AND WHAT DID YOU DO in the Grand Slam, Daddy? When England's front row reflect on this question in say ten years' time, they needn't be reticent about their contribution. By 2001, Jeff Probyn will be working hard in the family furniture business and enjoying a little weekend sailing. Brian Moore will be devoting his considerable energies to blazing a lucrative trail in the world of corporate finance and Jason Leonard could be the world's most capped player. At 32, he'll just be approaching his prime!

Their roles throughout the Grand Slam were crucial because rugby will always be an intrinsically physical game and nowhere is the element of raw confrontation more exposed than the front row. It's where the battle begins, from the moment the packs first engage, and it's where the war is invariably won. Entire campaigns can be successfully conducted without wings but a side lacking a competitive front row is automatically condemned to a rearguard action.

Of course, the modern-day front-row player has to contribute elsewhere, including the loose. The hooker's line-out throwing is vital and a prop's support of his line-out jumpers is an art form in itself. But at the heart of their effort remains the scrum.

England's Grand Slam trio, like the team in general, present an interesting contrast in styles, not to mention dates of birth and occupations. The youthful Leonard, all determined concentration and honest toil. The voluble Moore, full of noisy commitment and passion. And the sanguine Probyn, a highly individualistic but consummate craftsman going quietly about his business.

They finished the Five Nations' campaign as an impressively integrated unit, but back in September England's front row was one of the few volatile areas of selection in an otherwise enviably settled squad. Paul Rendall, you will recall, had done a splendid job at loosehead the previous season and, despite the march of time, the 'Judge' was looking fit and keen to extend his international career. As one of England's senior players, Rendall was spared the necessity of touring Argentina last summer, which allowed Leonard to seize his opportunity with two impressive Test performances. A new contender had emerged from nowhere.

Moore insisted on travelling to Argentina, despite a crushing schedule during the previous 18 months which included a significant contribution to the successful 1989 Lions tour of Australia. By his own admission he was feeling jaded and back in Britain he faced the additional stresses of starting a new job in London, moving house and finding his feet at Harlequins.

So it was the combative, ever-reliable John Olver who played for England against the Barbarians and subsequently won his first cap against Argentina at Twickenham in November. Jason Leonard made his home 'Test' debut that afternoon, leaving Probyn as the sole front-row survivor from the traumatic afternoon at Murrayfield eight months earlier when Scotland clinched their Grand Slam.

Gradually the situation resolved itself. The England selectors, looking forward to the World Cup, were prepared to gamble with Leonard's enormous potential at loosehead. At the same time they acknowledged Rendall's continuing excellence in the tight by retaining the Wasps man in the squad.

At hooker it was Moore, gradually regaining fitness and form, who got the vote over Olver. The England management are great believers in continuity and loyalty and their Grand Slam achievement provides an eloquent argument for such an approach. So Leonard, Moore and Probyn lined up against Wales in Cardiff, where they gave probably their least commanding scrummaging performance. Indeed Wales, on one notable occasion, even managed to shunt England backwards when a pushover try seemed inevitable. 'Our timing wasn't quite there and we were still short on practice,' recalls Probyn. 'But we were never remotely in trouble, we just didn't dominate like we should.'

A much stronger performance followed against Scotland, a forward encounter which featured a lively individual tussle between Probyn and David Sole, two of the canniest forwards in world rugby. Sole has always taken exception to Probyn's low scrummaging style and at Twickenham the Scottish captain evolved a plan to 'upset Probyn's right foot'. Probyn was not impressed and has subsequently called on the law-makers to act before serious injury occurs.

Notwithstanding the entertaining Sole-Probyn sideshow, England looked ominously secure in the scrums, which established the platform for Rob Andrew ruthlessly to pin the Scots back with his kicking. Against Ireland, England suffered initially from their tactical fixation with wheeling, but once they concentrated on keeping the scrum straight and wearing their opponents

JEFF PROBYN, BRIAN MOORE AND JASON LEONARD: AN INTERESTING CONTRAST IN STYLES

down, normal service was resumed. And the decider against France saw their most complete performance, with the scrum rock-solid from the outset.

For Probyn, England's 21–19 win was an immensely satisfying moment after a long rugby apprenticeship which has included spells at Old Albanians, Ilford Wanderers, Streatham & Croydon, Richmond and finally Wasps. He made his debut against France in 1988, at the age of 31, and describes his international career as 'Cinderella-like'.

'I didn't emerge from any of the established stables like England Schools, England Colts or the student representative sides. But I learned in a hard school and when I made the England team I was always confident of my ability.' In fact, during the early stages of his career he often played at loosehead, and that proved a useful experience when assessing prospective opponents.

In 1987, Probyn travelled with the England squad to Australia and New Zealand for the World Cup but, along with Dave Egerton, was unlucky enough not to get a game. The memory lingers and, barring injury or ill-health, he intends to conduct a protracted campaign on England's behalf in the autumn. By common consent he was also unlucky to miss out on the 1989 Lions trip, having temporarily lost his England place to Gareth Chilcott after getting concussed against Ireland in Dublin.

Probyn's influence on Leonard, the youthful prodigy making his way in international rugby, has been more supportive than technical. 'I'm not a great believer in offering masses of technical advice. Every player has his own individual style and what suits one will not suit another – myself being the classic example. During training, the "Judge" gave Jason some useful tips, especially about line-out positioning, but on the field my main concern was to keep him concentrating. If you stop thinking during big internationals you stop playing. It's as simple as that. By keeping cool, Jason was able to maximise his playing potential.'

Probyn has painful first-hand experience of a young prop losing his cool – Federico Mendez, who disgraced himself playing for Argentina against England at Twickenham last November. Mendez crudely grabbed Probyn's groin before flattening Paul Ackford with a haymaker and being sent off.

Leonard began his meteoric career with Barking and Eastern Counties Colts and was soon invited to Saracens by Tony Russ, now technical director at Leicester. 'We knew immediately that Jason was something special,' says Russ. 'He had all the physical attributes and his attitude was superb. On a cold wet night at training Jason would work ferociously and inspire those around him. Yes, I was surprised by his immediate promotion to the England senior side but nothing he achieves in the future will surprise me.'

A Colts cap in 1987 was followed two years later by inclusion in the England Under-21 squad against Romania in Bucharest. The following summer came his big break in Argentina, where he displayed his mental toughness by raising his game above the general level of mediocrity.

JASON LEONARD: ALL DETERMINED CONCENTRATION AND HONEST TOIL

On returning to England, the Cockney from Barking moved to star-studded Harlequins. Saracens were not amused, having lost the promising Dean Ryan to Wasps the previous season, but peace soon broke out and Leonard's England shirt now hangs proudly in Saracens' Southgate clubhouse.

Leonard is intensely proud about playing for England, proof that the Celtic nations don't have a monopoly on passion and love of country. 'Jeff Probyn told me before my debut in Argentina that I was playing for my country, family, friends and every player who ever dreamt of pulling on an England shirt,' recalls Leonard. 'That's a big responsibility, but I find everything about representing England a great honour.'

By the season's end, Leonard looked completely at home in England's number one shirt, his youth and comparative lack of experience rarely proving a handicap. 'I was extremely impressed,' says the former England and Lions prop Fran Cotton. 'Jason made the transition to international rugby wonderfully well and if he continues to learn and develop he should be a powerhouse in the England pack for years to come.'

At 29, Moore should also be a key figure for a few years yet, given his devotion to physical fitness and the tendency of most hookers towards longevity. Moore has been at the heart of England's revival over the last three years, a determined, passionate character prepared to work hard at every aspect of his game.

Intelligent and outspoken, he is sometimes billed as the England shop-steward and it can be safely predicted that Moore's retirement years will not be spent as an RFU committee man. He talks from the heart, always seeing rugby as a player's game, and is prepared to argue the point whenever called upon.

The memory of that climactic finale at Twickenham still burns strongly: 'You looked out of the window of the coach as we drove in from Richmond and saw more people than usual milling around. They were more vocal. When you got into the ground and on to the pitch you felt the expectation coming off the terraces. It was a completely unique feeling. There's no fear of failure now but England is a side not satisfied with itself. The Grand Slam is nice but the World Cup is more important.'

Moore first came to prominence in 1982 when playing for England Students against the Fijians and later that season he toured Romania, Italy and Spain with the England Under-23 team. In 1983, he toured the Far East with the Students and two years later he captained England B on his debut against Italy. A non-cap appearance for an England XV against Japan in October 1986 confirmed his growing reputation and later that season he made an impressive England debut at Twickenham helping defeat Scotland 21–12. Since then, he has missed just one capped international – that game against Argentina when Olver was preferred.

His pace around the pitch has always been a startling feature of his game, while his pin-point line-out throwing to Dooley, Ackford and Richards is

BRIAN MOORE HAS BEEN AT THE HEART OF ENGLAND'S REVIVAL OVER THE LAST THREE YEARS

PROBYN, MOORE AND LEONARD: UNSUNG HEROES NOW MAKING THE HEADLINES

another big plus. And, of course, his primary scrummaging duties are never ignored, his striking remains quick and authoritative.

The front-row union are traditionally the unsung heroes of any side, but rugby's expanding profile is beginning to change all that. As column inches and airtime increase, our depth of understanding about their specific roles does likewise. Indeed, unsung heroes are not making the headlines the world over. In the United States one of the biggest names in American Football is Lawrence Taylor of the New York Giants, who actually plays in the unglamorous position of linebacker. In Australia, cricketer Merv Hughes has made a considerable fortune out of being an unsung hero and a regular guy.

Perhaps we're entering a new era of 'donkey' awareness, to borrow Barry John's descriptive phrase of his hard-working forwards. And why not? Front-row stars are often ripe characters with strangely photogenic qualities. And they can attract adulation. Were the Pontypool front row not immortalised in song?

Messrs Leonard, Moore and Probyn will have to struggle on without musical accolades, or indeed invitations to appear on *Wogan* like their illustrious skipper. But they have star quality and their efforts are greatly appreciated by England supporters everywhere.

Chapter Fourteen

HESLOP WINGS IN

By GRAHAM TAIT

GRAND SLAMS AND INTERNATIONAL CAPS were but a foreign language to Nigel Heslop not much more than a couple of years ago as the Lancashire wing decided the time had come to raise his ambitions. He duly moved across Merseyside from Waterloo to Orrell.

Though not an easy decision to make, it turned out to be just about the most important of his life. Accepting the current structure of club rugby in England, it is highly unlikely that this amiable policeman would have figured in the plans of Geoff Cooke, the England manager. Second Division rugby has become a poor base from which to gain access into the national side. 'I had many regrets at leaving Blundellsands,' explained England's new right wing, 'but I'm afraid it just had to be, I couldn't put off the decision any longer.'

Heslop, now 27, is no spritely one-day wonder from the junior ranks. He has worked for recognition at the top level, learning to combine his natural speed and talents with the deeper skills of becoming something of an all-rounder. He is now far more conversant with the finer arts of the game.

Gone are the days when pace was sufficient for a wing to reach the top. Solid defence, confidence under the high ball and the ability to stay on one's feet, even under the greatest pressure, are crucial ingredients of a wing's armoury. He must not seem to be vulnerable when the ball is with the opposition. It is these skills that have been nurtured and lately matured in the steamy tension of Orrell's Courage One and Pilkington Cup programme. Any weaknesses are instantly seized upon by the opposing half backs.

While the League has demanded greater fitness and determination it has also encouraged a lot of homework, the senior teams always probing and exploring for any aspect of the other team's game that can be exploited.

'Don't believe anybody who tells you they actually enjoy being under a high ball. They don't. But the more consistently you can deal with them, preferably turning a defensive situation into an attacking one, then the less you are likely to get aimed at you,' added Heslop.

It is perhaps appropriate that Heslop has made the right-wing position his own this past 12 months, for on England's last Grand Slam success it was also an Orrell man who wore the number 14 shirt, John Carleton scoring a hat-trick of tries on that famous afternoon at Murrayfield 11 years ago. In an era when Northern players provided the nucleus of England teams, Liverpool's Mike Slemen was on the other wing to provide the ideal balance – Carleton, the explosive runner, and Slemen, the complete footballer in anybody's language.

Heslop's style is probably somewhere between the two. Perhaps not quite as powerful a runner as Carleton, his all-round game more than makes up, though Heslop would be the first to accept that Slemen had the edge in defence, as he had over any wing during his entire career. It is perhaps ironic that though Heslop is now playing for Carleton's old club his career started with that of Slemen, the former Liverpool club down at the now forsaken St Michael's ground.

He played with Liverpool for a year, his first in senior rugby after leaving Rainford High School near St Helens. In that season he first came face to face with his colleague on the opposite wing, Rory Underwood. Heslop remembers that encounter: 'I'd been told he was quick, but it's not until you actually see somebody at close quarters that you accept the fact. He was a bit sharp that day. Mind you, he still is.'

After one season at St Michael's, Heslop switched to nearby Waterloo. But, following a promising spell, the decision to leave Blundellsands had to be made. 'Basically, I did not get enough opportunities to run with the ball and the opportunity of playing in Division One was just too great to miss. I had to go.'

One can sympathise with his reasoning, for Waterloo were heavily committed to a game built round their powerful pack at the time and to make best use of Heslop's skills they frequently selected him in the centre. Though one could see the logic, it was not in the player's best interests. So it was off to Edge Hall Road, where he came under the umbrella of Des Seabrook, one of the country's more resourceful coaches.

The first hint of international recognition came at the end of that first season with Orrell when he was selected for the England B tour of Spain. Of the current international XV, Heslop is the only member who went on that ten-day trip. To reach the senior team, there were still a few I's to dot and T's to cross before the finished object emerged at the end of another season with Orrell. Then it was off to Argentina with a depleted England party. Though it was not universally popular, before, during or after, that tour saw Heslop play in both internationals and he had one foot firmly in the door for the coming season.

It is a long way from the naturally friendly atmosphere at Orrell to the

NIGEL HESLOP HAS JUST SCORED

HESLOP ENCOUNTERS MICHEL TACHDJIAN OF FRANCE

even more naturally unfriendly crowds of South America. That was where he acclimatised himself to playing under pressure. England were still far from being the most popular nation in Argentina, for obvious reasons, and many of the younger players found it difficult to relax in the hostile atmosphere. But it provided Heslop with the opportunity to graduate with honours. The key to a good performance on that tour was the ability to relax, as best one could. Watching the senior members of the party, Heslop learnt to control his emotions, take each event as it comes and get on with the job.

From then, via a rare, short holiday, it was back to Orrell and their most successful season. The Lancashire club, though widely regarded as having just about the best pack in the country, do not have any representatives in the England eight. That fact is not lost on the stalwarts in central Lancashire who have their own views on the subject, but at the end of the day the Orrell forwards provide plenty of ball, and they are not afraid to use it. Those who have branded them a ten-man team would not get Heslop's support. 'We spin the ball round as much as anybody and, believe me, it is a pleasure to play behind such a pack. They give us backs plenty of opportunities.'

At the time of the Grand Slam, Orrell had chalked up more points than any other side in Courage One, had scored more tries and possessed the best defensive record. Not bad for the country's most famous 'lay-by'.

But while Heslop is full of praise for his team-mates and Des Seabrook, he insists that one must be happy and feel secure at a rugby club. There are other aspects to an establishment than just on the field. Typical of many clubs in the North, there is a relaxed family atmosphere about the place. Heslop is only too well aware of rugby's demands that affect family life, which is why the club plays such a fundamental role. 'My wife, Denise, is very understanding but it helps when she can go down to Orrell and relax, not just because I'm there but because she too feels a part of the place.'

Such are the demands of rugby and his job as a policeman in nearby Newton-le-Willows that, like most members of the England squad, he has little time for other activities. 'Basically, my spare time is nil. I just don't have any. It took us ages to book a holiday last year. Nobody would believe how difficult it was to fit it in. But I was determined to have one, otherwise you just get stale and then your game goes.'

Rugby has been good to Heslop, but his success has been hard-earned. A willing learner, he has come a long way from those early days. And most of it he has done himself, though no Orrell player's career is complete without some form of instruction from Seabrook and his hard-working backroom team. 'Des and his colleagues always have time for everybody, no matter their position. There is always scope for improvement and, if Des sees something in the context of a game that would be beneficial to anybody, he simply takes them aside and suggests they work on it. In a way I suppose I'm one of the outsiders, but Orrell are pretty much a home-grown unit. So, to have achieved the success they have managed, there must be a lot of hard work behind the scenes.'

A naturally friendly, unassuming young man, Heslop is deservedly proud of following in the exact footsteps of Carleton and is more than aware that his success reflects great credit on the North's leading club. Following their domination of the national side a decade ago, Northern clubs have enjoyed little success at the top level of late. Heslop's efforts are just another step in the right direction.

Chapter Fifteen

NO SWEAT
Jeremy Guscott

By DAVID LLEWELLYN

JEREMY GUSCOTT DOES NOT UNDERSTAND what all the fuss was about. England won in Wales in his first Five Nations' match in Cardiff and completed the Grand Slam in his second season in the tournament. 'What we have achieved is very hard to explain,' says the 25-year-old Guscott, who now has 11 England caps to his name. 'The Grand Slam, in a way, means more to the likes of Wade Dooley, Richard Hill, Peter Winterbottom, Rory Underwood and Rob Andrew, all the guys who have been playing for six, seven or eight seasons. To me it's only my second Championship. People like myself, Jason Leonard and Nigel Heslop sometimes wonder what all the fuss is about because we've come in and been fortunate to win it so soon in our international careers.

'It's like the Wales thing. All the kerfuffle about 28 years without victory meant nothing to the likes of us youngsters. We weren't even born when England last won. And anyway, I was quite used to going over the Severn Bridge with Bath and beating the top Welsh sides. I think the ending of the Cardiff hoodoo gave all those supporters who had traipsed into Wales since 1965 and watched those 13 defeats a sense of relief. It also gave them a sense of achievement, of satisfaction that they would not have to take any more stick. And again for the players who have gone over there and lost three or four times, yes it was great. I'm not saying it wasn't special for me, but there was no history in it from my point of view. That's not to take anything away from what England did, but I've now been to Wales once as an England player and we won. End of story.'

But Guscott is not insensitive. When the final whistle sounded at Twickenham and French heads dropped, Guscott admits: 'My feeling was one of relief. Like the other guys in the squad. The pressure was off. We had done it. You see once again at the start of the season everyone was saying that we were going to win everything, so immediately the pressure was on. And

GUSCOTT TAKES OFF

JEREMY GUSCOTT: 'I USED TO PRETEND I WAS PELE. AND I ALWAYS WANTED TO PLAY A HERO'S ROLE FOR ENGLAND AS A FOOTBALLER'

we felt it through every single game. I remember talking to Grant Fox when New Zealand came over and played the Barbarians. He said he always feels sick before a match because he is so frightened of losing and he said after the last match, "I'm just glad the tour is over now and we've come through unbeaten." I now know what he meant. I don't feel it quite so intensely. It was nice to win and I was expecting the changing-room afterwards to be full of emotion and champagne, but it was very quiet – not as bad as it was after Wales, but still quiet, I think because we were drained.

'It is comforting, though, knowing we'd achieved what everyone expected us to do and, more importantly, what we knew we could do. It's there now. No one can take it away from us. We are the new team people are going to be talking about . . . until the next disaster. Let's hope it's not another 11 years before England next win the Grand Slam.'

The problem for Guscott and the rest of the England squad is that this is just the beginning. They now have the rest of the year, and more, to get through. The next 12 months contain a tough-looking tour to Australia, World Cup warm-ups, the tournament itself, followed by next year's Five Nations' Championship and no doubt another summer tour. 'It is an intense year for all of us in the England squad,' Guscott acknowledges. 'I remember, last January, Geoff Cooke telling us there was only 18 months to the World Cup and I thought about all the hard work that went in the middle. In fact, I missed last year's tour to Argentina because I was getting married. That was a bonus. But this time we've got that hard, physical tour of Australia, which will be very demanding on the body, what with the hard ground and the way they tackle over there.'

And Australia, of course, was where it all started. Well, nearly. There was the hat-trick for England on his debut against Romania in May 1989. That earned Guscott his Lions place in the same year. When he made his debut for them in the second Test against the Wallabies he proved to be a roaring success. The brilliance of his try, which turned the game and helped swing the series, captured the public imagination. Suddenly people spoke of Guscott's vision. His grace and pace earned the plaudits of every discerning fan.

As an established member of a talented England back line, the trainee public relations executive underlined his worth with half a dozen more tries in his next five England games, the pleasure of such a scoring feat being tempered by unexpected defeat in the Calcutta Cup to hand the Grand Slam glory to Scotland last year. This season, the emphasis was switched. The backs were put on hold and left to show another aspect of their game – defence. Needless to say, Guscott proved no sluggard in that department.

When France scored their outrageous opening try in the 13th minute of the classic Grand Slam encounter at Twickenham they drew gasps of astonishment from the crowd and no doubt the television audience at home. But Guscott's view of the moment was more down to earth. 'I didn't see a lot of it,' he admits. 'That's because I went up and tackled Serge Blanco. And I made sure

I kept hold of him so he couldn't contribute in support. The next thing I knew I was chasing back while Philippe Saint-André was going under the posts. I made a last-ditch effort to get him, but all I caught was one of his studs on my forehead. However, I'm impressed with the try now. I can sit back and watch it knowing we win in the end. I didn't appreciate the skills of Didier Camberabero until I watched it afterwards. It's just magic.'

Bearing in mind that Guscott himself is quite capable of such moments of magic, did it bother him that in this season's Championship he was not given the opportunity to use his handling and running skills? 'I didn't find it frustrating,' he maintains. 'I admit that to express myself best I need to have the ball in my hands and acres of space in which to run, but the opportunities at the top level in rugby don't come along all that often. This season England have played a more forward-oriented game. It wasn't conscious or calculated. It's just the way the games have turned out, purely because we have the strength there. There's been no real resistance from the opposition to stem the forward force that we generate. Since we were on to a winning thing I cannot see any reason for changing that. It's just like in business. If you make a profit by doing something in a certain way then you are not going to change it.'

But Guscott insists: 'As a squad, we know that we can play any style of rugby we choose. And, having that knowledge, that self-belief, is adding more to the confidence of the squad. It doesn't mean England are going to play a more expansive game in the World Cup. It is impossible to predict the way we will play. The game against the All Blacks will be a forward battle. We will adapt accordingly. Against other sides the approach could well be different. The important thing is that we will be able to adapt. We know we can take on the best in the world and come out on top. We believe that.'

Guscott's certainty suggests someone who has harboured ambitions to succeed at the top level since first he handled a rugby ball, but that is not the case. It is true the young Guscott's boyhood dream was to play a star role for England in the World Cup. Sadly, it is one dream that must remain unfulfilled, because the sport concerned was soccer, not rugby.

'Football was what I dreamed about succeeding at,' he confesses. 'It was soccer's World Cup that caught my imagination. I used to pretend I was Pele. And I always wanted to play a hero's role for England as a footballer. I had no idea who was in the England rugby team in those days. From the moment I pulled on a shirt as a seven-year-old, playing mini-rugby at Bath, my ambitions in the game went no further than playing alongside the club's greats, people such as Johnny Horton and John Palmer. I certainly never had any fantasies about starring for England. In fact, even now, every time I pull on the blue, black and white of Bath, I love it. I would never want to stop playing for them. Without Bath, rugby isn't rugby for me.'

And there is something about international success and the demands it brings which bothers Guscott. As he looks ahead to the World Cup and beyond, he explains: 'After the World Cup we've got another Five Nations' tournament and that will no doubt be followed by another tour for England, and so it goes on. Eventually, what it boils down to is that we will be playing rugby all year round. There's no getting away from it. Pretty soon players are going to have to make sacrifices and I think in the end it is the clubs who are going to lose out. I've only turned out in League games for Bath this year. In the last eight weeks I've played twice for the club, which is unheard of for any Bath player. Before I became an international I'd have at least 30 games, if not more. Now I probably won't make 20.'

It isn't just international matches which are taking their toll of club appearances. As soon as the mud had dried after the French match, Guscott was packing his tropical gear and turning up for more training prior to flying out to take part in the Hong Kong Sevens as a member of the Barbarians squad. The trip meant missing Bath's Courage match at Nottingham, but Guscott explains: 'I haven't had the freedom in the Five Nations to express myself in the way I did last year. The Hong Kong Sevens is a pleasant way to finish the competitive season and perhaps show people a little of what they have been missing.' And in Guscott's case, a little is a lot.

Chapter Sixteen

A LEARNING CURVE
Richard Hill

By DAVID LLEWELLYN

AS FAR AS RICHARD HILL is concerned the Grand Slam could just as easily have been the sound of a door shutting once and for all on his rugby past. England's historic achievement finally exorcised the ghost of Cardiff, 1987.

'People said I looked serious coming off the field at Twickenham,' said Hill. 'I didn't mean to be, it was just that I was feeling very satisfied. A tremendous amount of work had gone into it on a personal level as well as from the team's point of view. I suppose I've felt all along that I had something to prove to everyone about my character after losing the England captaincy in 1987.'

Cardiff was just the start of it. Hill was held responsible by the authorities for the infamous brawl and not only lost the leadership, he was also banned for a match and in fact didn't return to the international fold until the World Cup later that year when he turned out against the United States.

'All through that following year I played badly,' explains Hill. 'I went through a funny stage. It would have been quite easy to have called it a day. I'd had a rough ride and hadn't really enjoyed playing for England. Matches then were not pleasant experiences. Then to get all that thrown in your face when you were trying as hard as you could, well, I suppose I could have turned around after that and said, "That's it".

'But in the summer after the World Cup I started reassessing what I wanted to do. Over the next several months I was making up my mind. It was May 1988 when I decided to have another go at it. I didn't know if I would get my England place back, but I desperately wanted to.'

That was not the turning point in Hill's career though. That didn't come until September of the same year when he was sent off against Harlequins for punching their scrum half Richard Moon. Hill willingly confesses: 'In all fairness I'd been a bit naughty before that and got away with quite a bit. I think I'd been lucky to stay on the field on several occasions before that incident. The trouble is, when you get away with it you continue to behave like that.

'But the worrying thing for me was that I had no idea, not even to this day, why I did it. It certainly wasn't premeditated. I just reacted, but to what? I really don't know. There were just a couple of minutes left. We'd won the game anyway and the whistle had gone for an infringement, when I belted Richard Moon and came close to inflicting serious injury. I punched him in the eye. It was really dangerous.

'I panicked then because I thought is this going to happen to me again? Am I going to go out with the best of intentions, vowing not to hit anyone then in the heat of the moment do precisely that? I was petrified because I knew that one more incident would mean England would never look at me again.'

And this was *the* turning point for Hill. 'For the next six months I made a conscious effort before games to calm myself down completely and all through every match I'd keep saying to myself, "Don't get involved here." I went overboard to be as nice as possible. People would tell me they saw me smiling in games – I don't smile quite as much now, but then I had to go right to the other extreme. I had to be as polite as I could to the opposing scrum half in every game.

'Another factor which helped me a lot, when I was so vulnerable to provocation, was that people, opponents, didn't take advantage of that. They could so easily have taken the opportunity to get me sent off in a big game and increase their side's chances of winning but no one did. There was no provocation whatsoever. I am really grateful to them for that.'

So the rehabilitation continued. During his time in the wilderness Hill worked on his skills, carrying out his by now legendary training routines of 200 passes, as well as endless kicks. 'I'm certainly a better player now than I was back then,' says Hill. 'I've concentrated on the skills and my game has improved. But I still had to prove to the England management that it was all behind me. I think they wanted a season to see if I had adopted a different outlook. I was told when I first came back, "You are on shaky ground because of your past."'

Twickenham, 4 November 1989 marked the comeback. Two players were sent off but neither of them was Hill. England beat Fiji comfortably, 58–23 and although Hill didn't score he passed his test and the management's test. That match also marked the fulfilment of a boyhood dream for the 29-year-old Hill.

'When I was at school the dream of being in an England team that won the Triple Crown or completed the Grand Slam was unthinkable,' says Hill. 'I had always wanted to play for England, don't get me wrong, but that was as far as it went. But David Egerton joined my school, Bishop Wordsworth's in Salisbury, and we played in the Schools XV. He did well for England Schools and I once watched him at Twickenham. He and I always used to think it would be fabulous to play in the same England team. We

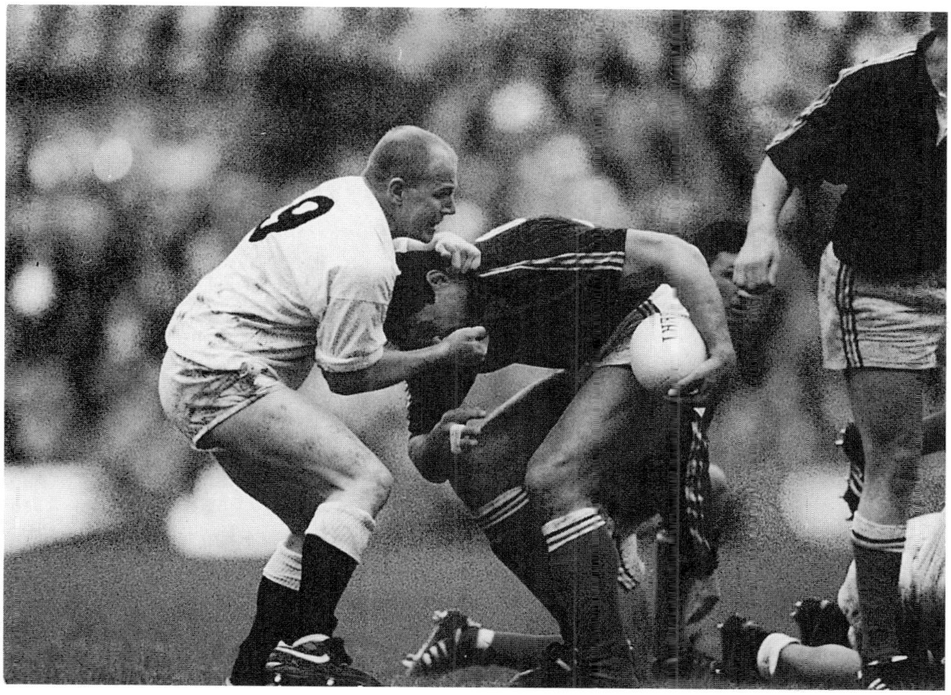

RICHARD HILL FELT HE HAD SOMETHING TO PROVE. HERE HE MAKES THE POINT TO MARC CECILLON OF FRANCE

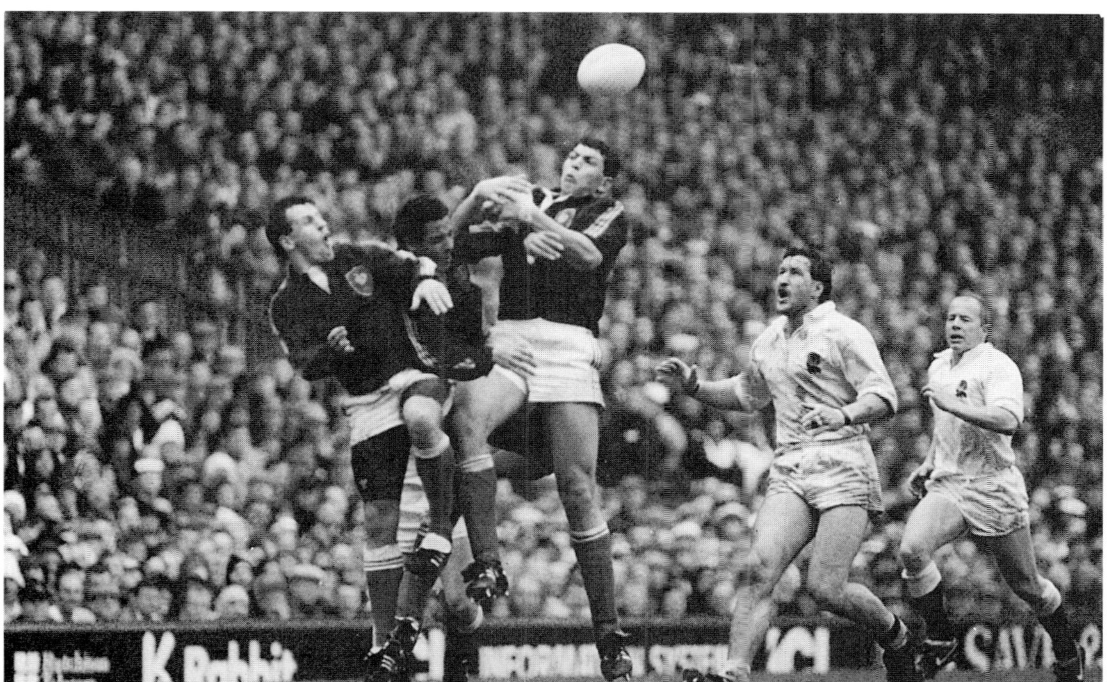

SAINT-ANDRE, BLANCO AND BENAZZI ARE ABOUT TO ENCOUNTER A LITTLE LOCAL DIFFICULTY FROM TEAGUE AND HILL

never thought it would come true, but it did. Against Fiji. That was a big moment for us.'

It was, as they say, the start of the rest of his international career. But if Hill were a selector he'd make it hard for himself to get into the side. 'I'm not one of the most talented scrum halves around,' he admits candidly. 'I've always had to work hard to keep up with everyone else.

'I rate Robert Jones of Wales very highly. Now he really does have a natural gift. He has it all. The skills, the dummy, the sidestep, a lot of things other scrum halves don't have. In addition he can pass and kick with great accuracy. He is a tremendous player. It's sad that he has lost his form, but he is still the best scrum half in Wales.

'Then there's Rob Saunders, who is also captain of Ireland. A difficult enough job in itself, and I can speak with authority on that. But considering he is only 22 he has done exceedingly well. He is very strong and does a lot of good work in a game. He has the potential to become a very good player.'

It doesn't seem to be modesty that prompts Hill to dismiss his obvious gifts and talk of his rivals. It is a genuine belief that he is a grafter with little natural talent. Perhaps his frustrated attempts to get into the England schoolboy set-up from Under-16 and up convinced him. When he finally got into England Colts he was understudy to Nigel Melville, whose own England career was scarred with, and eventually ended by, injury.

'I've had to put a lot more hours in than other people just to try to achieve the same as them,' Hill explains. 'My wife Karen will bear witness to the time rugby demands from me. For some people it is just enough to turn up at training twice or three times a week, whatever is required of them. They've got the natural gift, the speed or whatever, they don't need to work at it. Unfortunately I do.

'But for that reason I think winning the Grand Slam means so much more to me. I feel I can appreciate it to a greater degree. I was delighted. I think we all learned something from the last two attempts to win the Slam. I noticed throughout this season that the level of panic diminished with each match.

'Ireland was without doubt the hardest game. They broke up our rhythm more than any other team managed. When we played Wales we put a stranglehold on them. It was a similar story against Scotland, when we dominated territorially. You don't feel so much pressure when you are camped in the opposition's half. But the Irish gave us a lot of scary moments. Although we started well, they came back strongly, put a lot of high balls on us and rattled us. They didn't let us settle into our game plan and that was worrying.'

And so to Twickenham and France. All England expected a certain amount of expansion in their team's approach but Hill says: 'Throughout the season conditions have dictated the style; they have not been ideal for running rugby. But we make no excuses for playing the way we have done. We wanted to win.

'We would like to run the ball more, score more tries, but in the case of

HILL IN ACTION AGAINST WALES:
'. . . WE PUT A STRANGLEHOLD ON THEM'

the Grand Slam, winning is everything. Against France I was disappointed I didn't get a chance to run the ball all that often but the tactics didn't require that. It was up to our back row just to keep it in tight rather than pop the ball out to me so I could go round the sides.

'In fact we were able to drive straight through the middle of the French defence because they had men standing off on either side of the scrum looking for me to make a break. And when our forwards can drive like that staying on their feet then there's no real reason for me to have the ball. That drive has been described as a rolling maul but it isn't quite right. It's a skill that England have developed – we just move it a little bit to one side and then drive. I think the rolling maul is not such a good tactic because you tend to go sideways. What we have is more of a driving maul, where people focus on the ball and really go forward. It's a bit like a wedge, very All Black in style.'

Defensively Hill feels England excelled themselves this year. 'One pleasing aspect of the Five Nations' Championship was the fact that we didn't give many tries away. Until the France game anyway,' he adds ruefully. 'That try was very annoying. I think it was Nigel Heslop who made the comment at the team meeting before we left the hotel that morning. He said we had to remember to defend the same when the ball is behind the French goal-line as we would do if we were on our own 22. We all said, "Yeah, yeah, yeah" and thought it was a good point, but when it came to it, no one was switched on to what the French were up to and they did precisely what we'd discussed. As they charged towards our line I remembered those very words.

'I must admit I thought it was a bit ominous when they scored that try because we felt we'd had a very good start. We put pressure on them early in the game yet suddenly we found ourselves 6–3 down. A few alarm bells started to ring, but the composure returned and we got back into the game. As the match went on I don't think anybody really thought there was going to be much doubt about the outcome. There was obviously a chance there in the last couple of minutes but I think most people in the side were pretty confident that we'd win.

'Technically I think it was one of my best games for England. I didn't have cause for a great deal of running but in terms of the accuracy of my passing in the wet conditions and the precision of my kicking as well as my decision-making I think it must rank as one of my best games if not *the* best.

'And England have the best pack I've ever played behind. They have supplied some tremendous ball. I think, collectively, they must be one of the best packs England has ever produced. Obviously, in the past there have been some outstanding, world-class individual English forwards but never all eight at the same time.'

Hill's analytical brain and sharp eye did not focus solely on England's achievements. In their surge to the Grand Slam, 'this great prize' as Hill calls it, there were other stars.

'I think we were lucky Phil Davies wasn't in the Wales team that played us,' he says. 'When he was brought back he helped get their pack going in times of crisis. All right he's not the fastest thing on two legs, but he is strong, he's committed and he knows the game very well. He is street-wise and I think he stood out from what I saw of the Wales matches.'

Of the Scots, Hill singles out Gary Armstrong, at scrum half: 'He has had a superb Championship. He is very strong, very committed. I rate him very highly. And John Jeffrey, the flanker, is always a thorn in every side.'

Ireland fullback Jim Staples was another to catch Hill's eye. 'He impressed me. He doesn't look the part. He's a bit thin and gangly, but he really can motor and he tackles courageously. I like the look of him. And of course Simon Geoghegan, the wing, had a marvellous Championship. He seems to be able to go through anything. Allow him half a gap and he's through. Incredible. He's a very strong runner with a great future.'

As far as England go Hill is reluctant to single out any individual, understandably. 'It was a team effort,' he explains. 'But I think a couple of the newer boys deserve a mention. Nigel Heslop because it's great to have a wing who will chase all your kicks, good or bad, and try to make them something special. And prop Jason Leonard. He's only, what, 22? He's come through and answered all the critics by scrummaging against the best the other nations have to offer. He's doing really well.'

Which all bodes well for the World Cup this autumn. And Hill is optimistic about England's chances. Having laid the ghost of Cardiff, broken an unenviable sequence of defeats in Wales and put the 1980 Grand Slam firmly behind them, the pressure is off, Hill says. 'The Grand Slam is over. Now we have to gear ourselves up for the pre-season work. One major plus point of this Championship, bearing in mind we all wanted to run a bit more and score tries, is that having won everything this season there is still something to spare. I feel England can enter another dimension with their play. It would be a bit sad if having won the Championship in that sort of expansive style we then felt we had nowhere left to go. Players could well have been asking themselves, "How can we improve on that for the World Cup?" It would have been terrible if we had all thought we couldn't play much better and that the Championship had really stretched us, and I would have been worried.

'As it is I think we all know we finished with something to spare. We could play a lot better than we have done this season. We can expand our game, yet still maintain control. We can score more tries. We have some of the best finishers in the game.

'Having said that I know Jerry Guscott, although he is obviously disappointed at having seen so little of the ball, was still highly delighted to have won the Grand Slam. If it came down to a choice for him of scoring half a dozen tries as England lost or touching the ball ten times without crossing the line but England winning the Slam, he would prefer the latter. We all would. It was what we wanted. It is a fantastic feeling to have become a part of rugby history.'

It must also be good to know that some other things have been consigned to history.

RICHARD HILL IN ACTION AGAINST THE SCOTS. HE RATES GARY ARMSTRONG

RICHARD HILL: 'IT IS A FANTASTIC FEELING TO HAVE BECOME A PART OF RUGBY HISTORY'

Chapter Seventeen

WITHIN ARMS' REACH
Travels Along Route '63

By BARRIE FAIRALL

IN 1963 I WAS WORKING for the *Sunday Telegraph*, the weather so bad in the depths of winter that for weeks on end there was no rugby to report on unless you happened to live in the far South-West or had graduated to international-match status. Indeed, such was the intensity of the cold that for something like a fortnight I never once removed the old army blanket frozen to the bonnet of the Standard 8 I had purchased for the princely sum of £25 and 10 shillings.

Those were the days, and so they were for England. Years later, and now free-lancing with *The Independent*, I asked the old England wing Peter Jackson for his memories of that great Cardiff victory over the Welsh. Finally, 28 years further on, England at last triumphed again, the perfect start to their 1991 Grand Slam season and the hoodoo laid to rest.

The expeditionary force of '63 contained some hard and resourceful men. They had to be simply to survive, let alone achieve their objective in one of the most barren wastelands known to the modern generation of Englishmen who every two years since have turned up and attempted to emulate their illustrious predecessors.

It was a bitterly cold winter 28 years ago and yet those old-timers made light of the situation as they set off for the Arms Park and another crack at Wales. Low on expenses and yet high on morale, they picked up some protective clothing along the way and warmed the hearts of their supporters with straightforward winning rugby.

Over a quarter of a century later and England still expected. Would the Welsh, bar the one small hiccup of a 13-all draw in 1983, cease their biennial habit of destroying England's dreams or were the English condemned to living in the shadow of yesteryear?

'It was all so different then, you know,' said Peter Jackson, the will-o'-the-wisp wing in that rare English triumph. 'We met on the Friday lunchtime and because the grounds in Wales were so hard we went and trained on the beach at Porthcawl. You couldn't do a great deal and we simply played beach football.'

In the days when a coach was something you travelled to the match in, the game plan was purely basic. 'There were one or two older heads among us and it was more of a consensus of what we should do. We concentrated more on attack than what you could do if they attacked us. We had a very much more positive approach to those sort of things. We knew what we had to do from a defensive point of view and we more or less concentrated on how best to attack their back row.'

His enthusiasm and love of the game come over loud and clear. In his 61st year and having been forced to retire from business following a heart bypass operation, the commitment to rugby continues in the role of secretary – at his club Coventry and the Senior Clubs Association. He presses on with a proud winter's tale.

'We stopped on the way up from Porthcawl. The Rugby Football Union had made arrangements with Wolsey to supply us with something to wear under our jerseys and shorts. It was the first time that anything like that had ever been done. We were also given some woollen gloves. I used mine later in the garden, but not during the match – although I recollect that one or two players did by cutting off the fingers.

'As for the game, it was Malcolm Phillips making the first try that set us up. We were being pushed in our 25 and a long throw from Jim Roberts missed out Richard Sharp and went straight to Mike Weston. When I got the ball, as luck would have it, I hit a bit of soft ground which kept me running straight.

'Poor old Malcolm, meantime, was on the slippery slope but there was no doubt in my mind that P. B. Jackson wasn't going to round Hodgson, the Welsh fullback. But he committed himself to me and I can remember thinking, "Malcolm, where are you?"

'Eventually, he did get up to me and took the pass very well. Both Hodgson and I were left lying on the ground, he obviously hoping that two pursuing Welshmen would take Phillips, and me urging him on. So he scored the try and John Owen later got the second, while Sharp converted both and dropped a goal.'

England, with Sharp as captain, won 13–6. They had taken the field with seven new caps – which included the complete front five. 'When you come to think of it, that is pretty fantastic,' said Jackson. 'It is staggering when you consider things today, but in my first international in 1956 I think we had about ten new caps when they threw us into the Welsh cauldron.'

The memories of the 1963 victory continue to flood back. 'After the dinner, I can remember coming out of the Angel Hotel and being pelted with snowballs by a crowd of Welsh supporters and then we rushed out on the pavement and started throwing them back.'

WILL CARLING, THE FIRST MAN
SINCE R. A. W. SHARP TO LEAD
ENGLAND TO A CARDIFF TRIUMPH

ENGLAND

	15.	J. G. WILLCOX Oxford University
LEFT WING	11.	J. ROBERTS Sale
LEFT CENTRE	12.	M. P. WESTON Durham City
RIGHT CENTRE	13.	M. S. PHILLIPS Fylde
RIGHT WING	14.	P. B. JACKSON Coventry
STAND OFF	10.	R. A. W. SHARP Wasps (CAPTAIN)
SCRUM HALF	9.	†S. J. S. CLARKE Cambridge University
	1.	†N. J. DRAKE-LEE Cambridge University
	2.	†J. D. THORNE Bristol
	3.	†B. A. DOVEY Rosslyn Park
	4.	†A. M. DAVIS Torquay Athletic
	5.	†J. E. OWEN Coventry
	6.	†D. C. MANLEY Exeter
	8.	B. J. WIGHTMAN Coventry
	7.	D. P. ROGERS Bedford

Touch Judge: Mr R. A. B. CROWE (RFU)

† = capped

Roger Michaelson, the Welsh back-row forward, has a different story to tell. He won his first and only cap that day and it was a bit like the words of Oates to Scott on another expedition of yesteryear: 'I'm going outside and may be some time.' Michaelson said: 'We were obviously a bit choked. It happened so quickly and I thought we should have won it. We had about three scoring chances. Robert Morgan went over the line and was pulled back for not grounding the ball properly. Then David Watkins ran 70 yards up the field and Morgan dropped the pass. But the most glaring thing of all was Dewi Bebb's miss. He went clear, went to transfer the ball to his left-hand side and dropped it because it was so bloody cold.'

From Cardiff, England went on to win the Championship that year and now that situation has blossomed once again. 'Each match has to be played on its own merits,' said Jackson. 'You don't replace players of the quality of Jonathan Davies overnight and English team morale was pretty high.'

And as for Sharp, the last man before Will Carling to lead England to a Cardiff triumph: 'It was time England did it again and no one was happier than me when they did.'

THE CLASS OF '63

JOHN WILLCOX

BORN: *16 February 1937*

RUGBY CAREER – Caps: *16 (captain 3 times)* Position: *Fullback* Club: *Oxford University* Also played for: *Fylde, The Army, Harlequins, Paris University Club, Headingley* Retired: *1966*

PETER JACKSON

BORN: *22 September 1930*

RUGBY CAREER – Caps: *20* Position: *Right wing* Tries: *6* Club: *Coventry* Also played for: *Old Edwardians, The Army, Lions tour, 1959 (Australia and New Zealand)* Retired: *1964 (shoulder injury)*

MIKE WESTON

BORN: *21 August 1938*

RUGBY CAREER – Caps: *29* Position: *Left centre* Tries: *1* Club: *Durham City* Also played for: *Richmond, Lions tour, 1962 (South Africa) and 1966 (Australia and New Zealand)* Retired: *1969. England selector, 1976–87. Chairman of selectors, 1985–87. England manager, World Cup 1987. Played cricket for Durham, 1956–77 (batsman and spin bowler)*

MALCOLM PHILLIPS
BORN: *3 March 1936*
RUGBY CAREER – Caps: *25* Position: *Right centre* Tries: *5* Club: *Fylde* Also played for: *Oxford University, Devonport Services. Captain of Lancashire, 1962–65* Retired: *1971. England selector, 1976–79 and 1981–83. Chairman, North Division, 1989*

JIM ROBERTS
BORN: *25 June 1932*
RUGBY CAREER – Caps: *18* Position: *Left wing* Tries: *6* Club: *Sale* Also played for: *Cambridge University, Old Millhillians. Honorary secretary, Sale, 1962–66. Fixture secretary, Sale, 1962–71*

RICHARD SHARP
BORN: *9 September 1938*
RUGBY CAREER – Caps: *14 (captain 5 times)* Position: *Stand-off half* Tries: *2* Club: *Wasps* Also played for: *Redruth, Oxford University, Royal Navy, Bristol, Lions tour, 1962 (South Africa). Chairman of South-West Council for Sport and Recreation since 1984. Awarded OBE in 1986 for services to sport*

SIMON CLARKE
BORN: *2 April 1938*
RUGBY CAREER – Caps: *13 (debut in this match)* Position: *Scrum half* Tries: *1* Club: *Cambridge University* Also played for: *Hove, Royal Navy, Bath, Yokohama, Blackheath* Retired: *1987. Played cricket for Kent 2nd XI (opening bat and leg-spin bowler)*

NICK DRAKE-LEE
BORN: *7 April 1942*
RUGBY CAREER – Caps: *8 (debut in this match)* Position: *Loosehead prop* Tries: *1* Club: *Cambridge University* Also played for: *Kettering, Rosslyn Park, Leicester, Manchester, Waterloo* Retired: *1969 (back injury)*

BEV DOVEY
BORN: *24 October 1938*
RUGBY CAREER – Caps: 2 Position: *Tighthead prop* Club: *Rosslyn Park* Also played for: *Lydney, Cambridge University, Roundhay, Bristol* Retired: *1976. Headmaster, Leeds Comprehensive. Head of sport and recreation, Millfield School, since 1982*

MIKE DAVIS
BORN: *23 January 1942*
RUGBY CAREER – Caps: *16 (debut in this match)* Position: *Second row* Club: *Torquay Athletic* Also played for: *St Luke's College, Royal Navy, US Portsmouth, Harlequins* Retired: *1972. Coach, England Under-15, 1970–72 and Under-19, 1973–78. England coach, 1979–83*

JOHN THORNE
BORN: *1 January 1934*
RUGBY CAREER – Caps: *3 (debut in this match)* Position: *Hooker* Club: *Bristol* Also played for: *Cleve* Retired: *1966*

JOHN OWEN
BORN: *21 September 1939*
RUGBY CAREER – Caps: *14 (debut in this match)* Position: *Second row* Tries: *1* Club: *Coventry* Also played for: *Cambridge University, Blackheath, Moseley*

DICK MANLEY
BORN: *17 February 1932*
RUGBY CAREER – Caps: *4 (debut in this match)* Position: *Blind-side flanker* Club: *Exeter* Also played for: *The Army* Retired: *1963*

BRIAN WIGHTMAN
BORN: *23 September 1936*
RUGBY CAREER – Caps: 5 Position: *number eight* Club: *Coventry* Also played for: *Old Edwardians, Moseley, Rosslyn Park. Emigrated to Canada, 1964. Played for British Columbia v New Zealand, 1967. Lived in Fiji, 1970–87. Coach of Fiji team which won Hong Kong Sevens, 1977. Assistant secretary, Fiji RFU for ten years. Vice-president of Oceania Olympic committee, 1981. Vice-president of Oceania Commonwealth Games Federation, 1982. Moved to Tonga, 1987*

BUDGE ROGERS
BORN: *20 June 1939*
RUGBY CAREER – Caps: *34 (captain seven times)* Position: *Open-side flanker* Tries: *3* Club: *Bedford Lions tour, 1962 (South Africa)* Retired: *1976. England selector, 1976–83. Chairman of selectors, 1980. Member of Mallaby and Barbarians committees. OBE for services to rugby*

Chapter Eighteen

PLAYER PROFILES

By BARRIE FAIRALL

WILL CARLING: *Harlequins, centre*
Born: *12 December 1965, Bradford-on-Avon, Wiltshire*
Height: *5ft 11in*
Weight: *13st 10lb*
Caps: *24, first against France, 1988*
Education: *Sedbergh and Durham University*
Occupation: *Has formed own company, Inspirational Horizons*

William David Charles Carling took over the England captaincy for the match against Australia in November 1988 and has now led his country 17 times. Destined now to lead England in this year's World Cup, which opens when England take on New Zealand at Twickenham on 3 October, for Carling the future beckons.

'Rugby means a lot to me,' says Carling. 'It is what I am good at, what I enjoy.' As for England's style of play in their Grand Slam season, Carling says: 'We have been amazed and hurt by the criticism and accusations that have come our way as winners. People say we have been negative and reverted to ten-man rugby . . . we want to be expansive within an organised pattern. We're more street-wise now.'

ENGLAND'S CAPTAIN, CARLING

SIMON HODGKINSON: *Nottingham, fullback*
Born: *15 December 1962, Bristol*
Height: *5ft 10in*
Weight: *12st 2lb*
Caps: *13, first against Romania, 1989*
Education: *Stamford and Trent Polytechnic*
Occupation: *Finance company employee*

Simon David Hodgkinson has been kicking England to victory ever since he marked his debut against Romania in Bucharest in 1989 with a haul of 19 points. Against Argentina at Twickenham earlier this season he was to register 23, an English scoring record which had stood since 1911. And so it continued, his seven penalties against Wales a world record. By the time he signed off against France at Twickenham with another 14 points, he had accumulated 64 to smash Lescarboura's record of 54 points in a Championship season – an average of 16 points a game.

'Many people thought,' says Hodgkinson, 'I might have been a stop-gap, but I have been able to take my chance. I expect to get every kick I take. It doesn't matter how near or far.' And Alan Davies, his coach at Nottingham, says: 'Simon is without doubt the best goal-kicker in the game.' High praise indeed for the man England have come to rely on.

SIMON HODGKINSON ON HIS WAY TO KICKING A WORLD RECORD SEVEN PENALTIES FOR ENGLAND AGAINST WALES

NIGEL HESLOP: *Orrell, wing*
Born: *4 December 1963, Hartlepool, Cleveland*
Height: *5ft 10in*
Weight: *12st 7lb*
Caps: *7, first against Argentina, 1990*
Education: *Rainford High School, St Helens*
Occupation: *Police Officer*

Nigel John Heslop was to benefit from the guidance of Mike Slemen, the former England wing and now B team coach, when playing for the Liverpool club. Now with Orrell, the Northern giants, Heslop's rugby career took off during last summer's tour of Argentina, where he played in both Tests in Buenos Aires.

'Basically,' says Heslop, 'I have good memories of the tour because I grew to know the rest of the squad really well. I don't think I have been as fit for a long time. Some people had mixed thoughts about the trip, but it came at the ideal time for me. I gained a lot of experience, not least that of playing in a crowded, hostile environment. I always used to get a bit wound up before a major game, but watching some of the older lads taught me how to stay calm. Relaxing is so important at the top level.'

NIGEL HESLOP BEATS ALEX MOORE OF SCOTLAND TO SCORE

JEREMY GUSCOTT: *Bath, centre*
Born: *7 July 1965, Bath*
Height: *6ft 1in*
Weight: *13st 3lb*
Caps: *11, first against Romania, 1989*
Education: *Ralph Allen CS, Bath*
Occupation: *Public Relations Officer*

Jeremy Clayton Guscott burst upon the international scene with a hat-trick of tries against Romania in Bucharest in 1989. On that day in May he was standing in for the injured Carling, something which he did when the England captain was forced to withdraw from the Lions tour of Australia that followed, Guscott winning two caps.

'I was always light, and wiry,' Guscott says, 'so I never was one of those juniors who could run the length of the pitch with about six little boys hanging off him. I had to jink about and do things my way. And when I was going into senior rugby I still didn't think I was powerful enough so I spent a long summer concentrating on my sprinting. Nine times out of ten I don't think about what I'm going to do, I just do it. That might be how Bath are so clever; they train you so that you go out there and do something in a match instinctively.'

JEREMY GUSCOTT INSTINCTIVELY TAKES ON THE MIGHT OF BLANCO

RORY UNDERWOOD: *Leicester, wing*
Born: *19 June 1963, Middlesbrough, Yorkshire*
Height: *5ft 9in*
Weight: *13st 5lb*
Caps: *43, first against Ireland, 1984*
Education: *Barnard Castle School, Durham*
Occupation: *Pilot, Royal Air Force*

Rory Underwood has had a glittering career with England, which began against the Irish in February 1984. He had progressed through the Colts, Under-23 and B teams, and has now equalled Tony Neary's record as the most capped England player of all time. RAF duties have restricted some tour appearances, but he won three caps for the Lions on the 1989 trip to Australia.

The fastest man in the England team – confirmed on the track during training weekends in Lanzarote – Underwood says: 'We are a well organised squad now and everyone knows what we intend to do in every area of the pitch. On top of that, confidence is high.'

RORY UNDERWOOD SWEEPS HOME FOR THE FIRST OF ENGLAND'S TWO TRIES AGAINST IRELAND

ROB ANDREW: *Wasps, outside half*
Born: *18 February 1963, Richmond, Yorkshire*
Height: *5ft 9in*
Weight: *12st 3lb*
Caps: *36, first against Romania, 1985*
Education: *Barnard Castle, Durham, and Cambridge University*
Occupation: *Chartered Surveyor*

Christopher Robert Andrew has now superseded the late W. J. A. Davies as England's most capped outside half after making his international debut against Romania in 1985. He scored 71 points in his first six England outings, including a haul of all 21 when Wales visited Twickenham in 1986. In 1989 he won two caps for the Lions after being flown out to Australia as replacement for the injured Paul Deans. A talented all-round sportsman, he has also captained Cambridge at cricket.

'I used to get myself worked up into a fair old state before international matches,' Andrew says. 'My decision-making was often criticised. Things were so bad at one time that I couldn't bear to look at the Sunday papers. It's fair to say the England selectors have been patient with me.'

ROB ANDREW CELEBRATES THE GRAND SLAM WITH A FEW THOUSAND OTHERS

RICHARD HILL: *Bath, scrum half*
Born: *4 May 1961, Birmingham*
Height: *5ft 7in*
Weight: *12st 3lb*
Caps: *21, first against South Africa, 1984*
Education: *Bishop Wordsworth's School, Salisbury, and Exeter University*
Occupation: *Financial Consultant*

Richard John Hill, after an absence of over two years, has now completed a run of a dozen successive internationals for England, having first been capped on the tour of South Africa in 1984. He has enjoyed great success with his club Bath, appearing in six of their winning Cup finals besides helping them to the first English League and Cup double.

A reformed character on the field, Hill says: 'I realised I was living a lie. I'm not that aggressive but I had gained a reputation and I was trying to live up to it. It was a nonsense. I hadn't even established myself in the England side when they made me captain and I couldn't handle it.' Dropped and disciplined in 1987, Hill now says: 'Now I'm not taking people on so much. I know now I'm of more value to a team keeping a low profile.' Certain in his own self-belief, Hill says: 'Now England believe in themselves.'

RICHARD HILL KICKS CLEAR FOR ENGLAND IN DUBLIN

JASON LEONARD: *Harlequins, loosehead prop*
Born: *14 August 1968, Barking, Essex*
Height: *5ft 10in*
Weight: *16st 8lb*
Caps: *7, first against Argentina, 1990*
Education: *Warren Comprehensive, Chadwell Heath*
Occupation: *Self-employed carpenter and joiner*

Jason Leonard made his first appearance for England during last summer's tour of Argentina when selected for the first Test in Buenos Aires. When playing for Barking, he was capped by England Colts. He subsequently joined Saracens and then moved on to Harlequins after returning from Argentina.

'Before my first international in Argentina,' says Leonard, 'Jeff Probyn reminded me I was playing for England, my family, friends, and every player who ever dreamed of pulling on an England shirt. That's a big responsibility.'

JASON LEONARD BREAKS THROUGH THE SCOTTISH LINE-OUT

BRIAN MOORE: *Harlequins, hooker*
Born: *11 January 1962, Birmingham*
Height: *5ft 9in*
Weight: *14st 2lb*
Caps: *29, first against Scotland, 1987*
Education: *Crossley & Porter HS, Halifax, and Nottingham University*
Occupation: *Corporate Financier, London*

Brian Christopher Moore made his England debut during the first World Cup when he appeared against Scotland. Missing from only two of England's last 30 internationals, he has also won three caps for the Lions when they toured Australia in 1989. Holder of a law degree, the former captain of Nottingham switched to Harlequins for the start of the season.

'Coming through such a physical ordeal and winning,' he says, 'brings a very deep sense of satisfaction. But it takes me three days to recover physically and mentally and feel balanced again. When people talk glibly about forward power they often underestimate the amount of effort and courage demands.'

BRIAN MOORE: DEEP SATISFACTION FROM A PHYSICAL ORDEAL

JEFF PROBYN: *Wasps, tighthead prop*
Born: *27 April 1956, London*
Height: *5ft 10½ in*
Weight: *15st 7lb*
Caps: *22, first against France, 1988*
Education: *London Nautical School*
Occupation: *Company director, reproduction furniture manufacturers*

Jeffrey Alan Probyn was a member of the English squad during the first World Cup in Australia, but did not gain a cap until the Paris international in January 1988. His education was designed to prepare him for a career in the Merchant Navy, though it was to his family's furniture-making business that he turned. In seafaring terms, however, Probyn is a keen yachtsman in his spare time.

Probyn was 31 before he arrived on the international rugby scene. 'During the big internationals,' he says, 'if you stop thinking, you stop playing effectively.' It was the teenage Argentinian prop Federico Mendez who stopped thinking in the Twickenham encounter with England last November, grabbing Probyn in the groin, laying out Paul Ackford and getting sent off. 'He really could be something special,' Probyn says, 'but he must channel that aggression.'

JEFF PROBYN, OUTNUMBERED THIS TIME

PAUL ACKFORD: *Harlequins, lock*
Born: *26 February 1958, Hanover, Germany*
Height: *6ft 6in*
Weight: *17st 6lb*
Caps: *16, first against Australia, 1988*
Education: *Plymouth College, Kent and Cambridge Universities*
Occupation: *Police Inspector*

Paul John Ackford has proved something of a late developer considering that he first represented the England B team over 11 years ago. Indeed, it was not until the Wallabies arrived at Twickenham in the November of 1988 that he first featured in a full international. Since then he has formed a formidable partnership with Wade Dooley, the twin peaks of line-out play in English rugby. Ackford has also won three caps for the Lions on the 1989 tour of Australia.

'I don't think I've improved all that much,' Ackford says, 'it's simply that when you are associated with a successful club and a London coach [Dick Best] whose bandwagon is really rolling, it makes an enormous difference. Of course, there's pleasure in turning out for Quins or London on a big occasion, but the pride and fervour you feel when you pull on that England shirt is indescribable.'

ACKFORD FEEDS RICHARD HILL, WITH A LITTLE HELP FROM HIS FRIENDS

WADE DOOLEY: *Preston Grasshoppers, lock*
Born: *2 October 1957, Warrington, Lancashire*
Height: *6ft 8in*
Weight: *17st 9lb*
Caps: *41, first against Romania, 1985*
Education: *Beaumont Secondary Technical School, Warrington*
Occupation: *Police Officer*

Wade Anthony Dooley is now England's most capped second-row forward, superseding Bill Beaumont's record during last summer's tour of Argentina. When he was at school, Dooley played rugby league. Since switching codes, though, and joining the Preston club, he has gone from strength to strength. Included in his list of achievements are two Lions caps won in the second and third Tests in Australia in 1989.

'Nowadays,' he says, 'I aim to play about 30-34 times in a season, but after the season when I first played for England I counted all the games I had played: internationals, divisionals, county, police and club. It came to 72 . . . I realised I was doing something wrong, so I set about structuring my season better . . . you get mentally and physically jaded if you do too much; if you want to peak for internationals you have to start thinking this way.'

WADE DOOLEY CHALLENGES DAMIAN CRONIN IN A LINE-OUT

MIKE TEAGUE: *Gloucester, flanker*
Born: *8 October 1959, Gloucester*
Height: *6ft 3in*
Weight: *16st 4lb*
Caps: *15, first against France, 1985*
Education: *Churchdown School, Gloucester*
Occupation: *Self-employed builder*

Michael Clive Teague toured South Africa with England in 1984, but did not win his first cap until the following year when he came on as a replacement for the injured John Hall against France. A Lion in Australia, where he gained two caps in 1989, Teague has had to shake off a persistent shoulder injury and fight for his place in the England side.

His beloved Kingsholm had to wait almost half a season before Teague returned from injury on the first day of January last year. 'It just feels good to pull on an England jersey again,' he said at the time. 'I started training again . . . with one aim in mind: to play again for England.' And his wish came true.

MIKE TEAGUE, IN THE CENTRE OF THE ACTION AS USUAL, GUARDS WHILE HILL CLEARS

DEAN RICHARDS: *Leicester, number eight*
Born: *11 July 1963, Nuneaton, Warwickshire*
Height: *6ft 3½ in*
Weight: *17st 3lb*
Caps: *25, first against Ireland, 1986*
Education: *John Cleveland College, Hinckley*
Occupation: *Police Officer*

Dean Richards marked his international debut, against Ireland at Twickenham in 1986, with two tries. His career, though, has been dogged by injury and he missed last winter's complete Five Nations' programme with shoulder trouble that was also to rule him out of the summer tour to Argentina. He did, however, win three caps for the Lions when they toured Australia in 1989.

Geoff Cooke, the England manager, once remarked that Richards need only to stand up to be in his team. 'He has an innate ability as a rugby player,' Cooke said. Richards, though, says: 'These expressions of confidence in me are a comfort in some ways, but I don't expect any special treatment; I still have to earn my place in the England team.'

DEAN RICHARDS LAUNCHES HIMSELF IN THE DIRECTION OF THE WELSH LINE

PETER WINTERBOTTOM: *Harlequins, flanker*
Born: *31 May 1960, Leeds*
Height: *6ft*
Weight: *14st 10lb*
Caps: *42, first against Australia, 1982*
Education: *Rossall, Fleetwood and Seale Hayne Agricultural College, Devon*
Occupation: *City of London Eurobond broker*

Peter John Winterbottom is now just one cap away from equalling Tony Neary's record as the most capped England forward. He has also won four caps as a Lion and played throughout the first World Cup in 1987. After missing the 1989 Championship, he returned to the fray for England in the crushing '89 victories over Romania and Fiji.

Looking to the future of the English side, Winterbottom says: 'It is a pity that five or six may go after the World Cup and a rebuilding job may have to be done. It would be far better for England rugby if most of the senior players went on because new blood could then slowly be brought in. It is much better for a team if you change a maximum of two positions in a single season.'

PETER WINTERBOTTOM FEEDS THE BALL BACK FOR ENGLAND IN DUBLIN

THE GRAND SLAM-WINNING TEAM

GRAND SLAM CELEBRATIONS

EPILOGUE

And so the journey ends, though others now beckon. First England visit Australia, a testing ground for great events come, the second staging of the World Cup.

Their preparations complete, England start the ball rolling when the All Blacks, holders of the Webb Ellis Trophy, roll into Twickenham on Thursday, 3 October. It is then that we will be able to judge just how much further down rugby's road England have travelled.